CAREER DEVELOPMENT FOR TEACHERS

Dedication
To Judith

Acknowledgement
I would like to thank Shirley, who continues to be an endless source of patience and good advice.

Second Edition

CAREER DEVELOPMENT FOR TEACHERS

Jim Donnelly

KOGAN
PAGE

First published in 1992
Second edition published in 2002

Kogan Page Limited
120 Pentonville Road
London N1 9JN
UK

Stylus Publications Inc.
22883 Quicksilver Drive
Stirling VA 20166–2012
USA

British Library Cataloguing in Publication Data

A CIP record for this book is available from the British Library.

ISBN 0 7494 3645 X

Typeset by Saxon Graphics Ltd, Derby
Printed and bound in Great Britain by Clays Ltd, St Ives plc

Contents

Preface   *vii*

1. **Career planning**   **1**
    Career objectives 1; Planning ahead – the new teacher 1;
    Personal strengths needed for teaching 2;
    Planning ahead – the experienced teacher 4;
    Money, status, self-fulfilment 5; A good school 6;
    Career appraisal and forward planning 9

2. **Job search**   **11**
    The newly qualified teacher 12; The move to middle
    management 14; Heading for the top 17

3. **Applying for posts**   **21**
    First step 21; Timetable 23

4. **Preparing a CV**   **27**
    Purpose 27; Basic information 28; First application 30;
    First steps to promotion 32; Primary deputy headship 36;
    Secondary deputy headship 38; Headship 42

5. **Getting an interview**   **49**
    Application form 49; Selection criteria 51; References and
    referees 51; Letters of application 53

6. **The interview**   **75**
    Invitation to interview 75; Pre-interview preparation 76;
    Getting there 78; Arrival 78; Tour of the school 79;
    The school ethos 81; Interview patterns 82; Interviews 88;
    Questions 91; Appointment 93; Debriefing 94;
    After the interview 94

Contents _____

7. **Development strategies**   **95**
Personal development 95; Professional development 96;
Performance managment 99; What does promotion
entail? 99; Summary 107

8. **Alternative routes into teaching**   **109**
Late entrants 109; Different routes into teaching 111;
Supply teaching 113; Secondments / interim management
114; Early retirement 115

Index   *117*

Preface

A lot has changed since the first edition of this book appeared in 1992. However, the essentials have not. The country needs, and its young people deserve, well-qualified and – above all – committed teachers.

The philosophy underlying this book is still that it is possible – in fact *necessary* – to plan your career in teaching. This should be done not only when you start but also at regular intervals throughout your career. Good fortune plays its part but at least you can plan to take advantage of such opportunities as they come along. Those who have a clear idea of what they get from teaching and know their objectives are more likely to recognize opportunities and to be in a position to seize them.

Now is possibly the best time for a long time to consider a career in teaching. Age is no longer the barrier it once was and it is possible to combine a short career in teaching with other careers. Training opportunities are better than ever before. Postgraduate training is much more practical, and less theoretical, than it used to be. There is an expectation that teachers will continue to learn throughout their time in the profession, rather than being expected to learn everything in the first year or two of teaching. Resources are being provided to pay for regular training and also for opportunities to visit other countries, to report on how they educate their young people. There are more non-teaching or support staff working in schools, supporting the work of the teacher. These include learning support assistants, administrative officers, home–school liaison officers and learning mentors. This helps take the burden from teachers and allows them to concentrate on becoming learning professionals.

The impact of ICT (Information and Communication Technology) on schools also means that there are many learning tools available to the teacher. The role is therefore changing from that of a teacher at the front of a classroom to a professional organizer of learning. The other thing to remember is that motivating young people to learn, and seeing them achieve because of your efforts, is a very rewarding occupation.

The demographic situation is encouraging for those who are looking to the future. A large proportion of the present teaching force is due to retire in the next 10 to 15 years, and they will need to be replaced. Many of these are in senior positions in schools.

Opportunities for secondments (for up to two years) have also become more common. There is a need for consultants for new initiatives and for teachers to work with local and national government departments on a short-term basis. These opportunities can help to offer a break from the classroom and provide an understanding of the 'bigger picture'.

Many teachers in the past entered the profession with a view to doing 40 years and then retiring with a pension. This pattern has broken down to some extent in recent years, and Chapter 8 deals with this situation. More teachers come into the profession at a later age and/or leave it before retirement age. It is also the case that schools are becoming more used to teachers taking a 'career break', particularly in the case of those (now both women and men) who may wish to spend some time out of the classroom, perhaps raising a family.

This book has been written for all teachers and gives examples for those at different stages of their careers. It may be easier if you plan your career from the outset but it is perfectly possible to take control even after some time in the profession. Each chapter deals specifically with one aspect of the ways in which jobs are advertised and appointments made, viewed from the unique standpoint of the teaching profession.

For the sake of simplicity, it is assumed throughout the book that promotion involves moving schools. However, the principles and practices outlined here also apply if you are looking for promotion within the same school. If you are thinking of promotion, it is a good idea to discuss this with the headteacher or another senior member of staff (deputy headteacher, head of department), prior to starting to make formal applications. If there are likely to be opportunities within the school in the future, this may the point at which you will learn about them.

1 *Career planning*

Career objectives

There are many barriers to achieving career objectives, some of which are beyond the individual's control. A school may close, ill health may strike, the school may go through a bad patch that makes it difficult to move, or personal circumstances may prevent one moving to take opportunities for promotion. However, one barrier that you can control is a lack of clarity about what your objectives are. For example, some people talk as if they would like to run a department in a secondary school or be a deputy head in a primary school, but their actions do not bear this out. They do not keep up with current trends through regularly reading leading journals, they do not attend courses, they do not actively examine the current job market; in short, they do not prepare themselves for such a move.

This is not to say that promotion is the only acceptable career choice – many teachers choose to concentrate on classroom teaching and do not wish to take on additional management responsibilities – but the purpose of this book is to ensure that this is a conscious decision and not something that 'just happens'.

Planning ahead – the new teacher

The first stage of career planning is to clarify objectives – to know what you want, not just from your career but also from your life. (This should also be done at regular, say five-yearly, intervals throughout your career.) If you are new to teaching you should write out your answers to the questions in the box below as a first step in thinking about your future.

Setting initial career objectives

1. Do I really want to teach? If so, what do I want to achieve as a teacher?
2. What are my present strengths? Will they be utilized in teaching?
3. What are my present weaknesses? Are they likely to make teaching very difficult?
4. What are the connections between my career and my personal life? Are they compatible?
5. What is the highest priority in my life at present? (For example, is it to teach a particular subject, to live in the same area, to be near relatives?)
6. Will I want promotion? If so, why? If not, why not?

The answer to the first question is the most important one. If you are in the initial stages of thinking about a career in teaching you need to know in detail what it is likely to involve. A good starting point will be your local school. Contact the head and ask if you can talk to him or her about your plans. Many will arrange for some observation time when you can see what a teacher's daily life is like. Of course, no two schools are alike so if you don't like the first one, you might try a second one before you finally make up your mind. It is also a good idea to talk to teachers you know already, who can give you an insight at least into their own school.

Personal strengths needed for teaching

If you wish to train to teach – or to start straight off under one of the government schemes – you are bound to be asked, 'Why do you want to teach?' Most teacher trainers or heads will expect a clear indication of a desire to work with children or young adults: the days when teaching posts were given to those who wanted to 'give it a whirl' are gone. You will almost certainly be motivated by a desire to increase opportunities for children: teaching is a 'caring' profession and you need to have that kind of orientation.

Analysing your strengths and weaknesses requires a degree of self-awareness and an ability to be honest with yourself. There is no point in choosing teaching if you do not really enjoy working with young people and cannot stand the stress of working all day in front of 25 or 30 pairs of eyes. In addition to liking to work with young people, you will also need stamina and determination – teaching is a lot more tiring than it looks!

Subject knowledge is necessary, as is a willingness to learn how to develop strategies for teaching in the classroom. There are many different theories of education, but in the classroom you must make it clear that you are going to take the responsibility for learning and exercise leadership: you will not last long otherwise.

Most careers impinge to a greater or lesser degree on one's private life and teaching is no exception. However, there are implications for your private life that are unique to this profession. If you live near the school you will be recognized when you are out shopping or going to a concert; your life will be less private than it would be in some careers. There are other more mundane – but expensive – drawbacks like having to take your holidays in the peak season. Society still expects that teachers will behave in certain ways. A visit by teachers to the pub at lunchtime can become a talking point in the local community, for instance, or the manner in which you dress outside school may cause comment. This may seem unfair but it is a fact of life.

Planning ahead – the experienced teacher

If you have already been teaching for some time, the box below contains some questions to help you focus your thoughts on resetting your objectives in the light of your present situation. As with the previous set of questions, you should write out the answers.

Resetting career objectives

1. What have I achieved in my present post?
2. What do I want to achieve in the future?
3. What are my present strengths? Will they be utilized in my intended post?
4. What are my present weaknesses? Will they cause a problem in my intended post?
5. Can I reconcile my plans with my personal life?
6. What is the highest priority in my life at present? (For example, is it to gain promotion? To live in the same area?)
7. Do I need a change? Does it have to be promotion?
8. Will this move limit my future possibilities?

The answers may differ considerably from when you first entered teaching. For example, you may find that in your present post you have achieved a lot that you did not anticipate. You will almost certainly have improved your teaching skills, and your training needs may now be geared more towards taking on departmental or school management responsibilities than on improving your classroom performance. Your personal life and priorities may be quite different, which will give rise to different career priorities. You may also feel that you need a new challenge, which may mean a change of school rather than taking on additional responsibilities in your present one.

Promotions nowadays almost invariably entail taking on some kind of management responsibility. You need to decide if you wish to do this. Very many teachers enjoy rewarding careers in teaching without such management responsibilities, while others would find this frustrating.

There have been recent government initiatives that affect the career prospects of teachers. These include the introduction of Advanced Skills Teachers, an upper pay spine (with what is effectively a bar after roughly five years of teaching) and assistant headteacher posts. This is dealt with in more detail in Chapter 7.

Money, status, self-fulfilment

A satisfying career offers money, status and self-fulfilment in varying degrees and every teacher needs to establish the relative importance of each one. If you do not confront these issues _you_ will not take charge of your career. While teaching can offer a degree of relative financial comfort, those who value money above everything else should find an alternative career or consider a move before they become 'locked in' to the profession. (This illustrates the importance of constantly revising one's objectives, since the importance of money can vary at different times in one's life.)

High status comes from a perception that others value the occupation concerned. Status is not a real phenomenon, more a psychological one. High status can therefore depend not only on where the school stands in the eyes of the local community and parents, but also can vary within one particular school.

Self-fulfilment is more difficult to quantify than money or, arguably, status. It comes from a sense of purpose and a feeling of achievement from one's daily work, much of which lies within the control of the individual school or college. In some ways, therefore, the most critical decision can be in choosing which schools to apply to.

A good school

While a good school can launch or develop a successful career, a poor one can blight it irreparably. It is important here to note that what constitutes a 'good' school to a prospective parent is not necessarily always a good school to teach in. It is possible to learn a lot in a school that is traditionally considered to be 'difficult', possibly because of its location. For a teacher wanting to learn, a good school will certainly have a good staff development policy, an ethos which encourages openness in sharing little problems (before they become big ones) and a sense of common purpose. The contributions of staff will be considered on their merits and not on their place in the hierarchy of the school.

This principle is equally applicable to both the large secondary school with 100 staff and the small primary school with perhaps half a dozen staff. In some ways a career in teaching is like chess: the first moves dictate to some extent how the whole game will unfold. A bad start does not necessarily mean that you will lose the game but it is obviously easier to win if your first steps are sound. OFSTED reports and the school's own Web site can give you an initial idea of whether a particular school is likely to appeal to you.

Choosing a school

Whether you are starting teaching or are at one of the important crossroads, there are some factors that are generally applicable when choosing a school. The factors shown in the box below need to be borne in mind when you are clarifying for yourself where you want to go.

Factors to consider when choosing a school

1. The age range of students – whether the school is primary, middle, secondary (with or without a sixth form) or FE.
2. Mixed or single-sex.
3. Geographical location.
4. Opportunities for promotion.
5. Selective or non-selective (for secondary schools).
6. Controlling body (eg LEA, grant-maintained, independent, denominational).
7. Compatibility with the ethos of the school (more will be said about this in Chapter 6).

Age range is very important. Personally I would find it difficult to cope with a class of 6-year-olds but others thrive on it. Some teachers like to teach A-level, while others prefer the 11–16 age range.

It is also important to ascertain whether you prefer to teach in a mixed or single-sex school. Most schools are mixed but there still are single-sex schools if you prefer to teach in one. (It is worth noting that teaching for a long period in a single-sex school could make moving into a mixed one difficult should you wish to; also, as there are fewer single-sex schools, there are fewer vacancies.)

The geographical location of the school may be important to you. However, it is fairly obvious that areas of rolling green fields are likely to have fewer children – and therefore fewer schools – than conurbations. Ease of getting to school is also important. This depends not only on distance but also on the infrastructure of the area.

Some schools offer greater promotion opportunities than others and this is certainly worth thinking about before you apply. A large school from which staff regularly go off to other posts may give chances of quicker advancement, whereas in a small school, particularly with falling pupil numbers, there may be fewer opportunities. One should bear in mind, however, that too many promotions within one school may hinder you later on, since you will lack the breadth of experience that is usually necessary if you decide to apply for a deputy headship or a headship.

While most schools are comprehensive, there are still selective schools (particularly in the private sector) and in many cases the geographical location of schools makes them selective in all but name. You have to make a decision about which type of school best suits you, bearing in mind your career objectives and your reasons for teaching. It is possible to move between the state and the private sector, but not many teachers do this.

Who controls the school can be an important consideration. If you work in an LEA (local education authority) school, there is likely to be greater uniformity in the way you are treated in terms of salary and conditions of service (although this has changed to some extent since the delegation to the governors of most of the employment powers previously held by the LEA). Independent schools can operate their own salary structures and conditions of service. If the school is a denominational one, it is important to bear in mind that you will be expected to subscribe, at least in broad terms, to its religious philosophy.

This leads on to the point about compatibility with the ethos of any school that you are considering. Some posts will require a person to fit in with existing ideas and plans, while others will require a lot of initiative. If you have a clear idea of your own strengths and preferences, you will be in a better position to decide if you match the post and the post matches you. There is enough anecdotal evidence of teachers who have thrived in one environment yet nearly given up in another to make the point that not all schools are the same.

There will be more detail on this in Chapter 6 when we come to look at preliminary visits and interviews, but before getting to this stage, one has to find a post and apply for it. The next chapter deals with this.

Career appraisal and forward planning

Once your personal appraisal is fully formed, you should use it to help focus your present and future development needs. Performance management now exists in all schools and should be used as part of your own self-appraisal process. It is an opportunity to have some external input into your decision-making and each part of the process should be seen as an opportunity, as a crossroads. Sometimes the road chosen may not matter much, but over the span of a teaching career there are certain choices that do matter. They are the ones that require a little thought and a little planning.

We will look in detail in the rest of the book at how to plan specific career moves. The general point to be made here, however, is that you should always be thinking about where you want to be in three years' time. Three years is the most commonly recognized length of time when one talks about 'recent experience', and if you apply for any job you will normally be asked to indicate recent experience, recent achievements and recent courses.

The advantage of thinking ahead is that you offer yourself choices. If you decide in three years' time that you do not want, after all, to go for a particular promotion you have prepared for, then at least you are exercising a genuine choice. If on the other hand you want to go for a particular promotion and find that you do not have recent relevant experience, then you may have denied yourself the chance of promotion at all.

2 *Job search*

Most schools advertise vacancies in the local press, and many LEAs also publish a regular list of internal vacancies. These sources are fine if you live in the area to which you wish to apply or know someone who does, but if not then you will need to rely on the national sources of vacancies. The *Times Educational Supplement* (TES) is still the market leader for teaching vacancies nationally, although some of the larger dailies also carry a selection, but if you are looking for temporary posts – to cover, say, a maternity leave – or for part-time posts, you will almost always have to look at the local sources. In recent years it is becoming more common to find vacancies advertised on the Internet. Jobs advertised in the TES also appear on its Web site, and you can download a ready-made application form (www.tes.org.uk). Other specialist organizations are also offering a vacancies and a curriculum vitae (CV) service.

It is vital to have a plan before starting your job search. Such a plan should have a timetable so that you have a clear idea, for example, of how long you are prepared to confine your search to your immediate locality. This applies whether you are looking for your first teaching job or your tenth. Teaching is unusual in that the vast majority of posts are filled in September, January or April. The custom of giving three months' notice for September resignations and two months' for the other terms means that there are three deadlines in the job applicant's year: these are 31 May, 31 October and 28/29 February (heads have to give an extra month's notice in each case), although in these days of cash-limited budgets and redundancies you may be able to persuade your present employer to let you leave without the required notice.

The timings of your action plan need to take account of more than resignation dates. If you are looking for your first post, your timescale is probably geared to getting a job as soon as possible. On the other hand if you are looking for a second post, perhaps with promotion in mind, you need to give careful thought to when you wish to move and when you are likely to be able to do so. It is never too early to think ahead when planning your career: as indicated previously, fate can sometimes hand you an opportunity or well-laid plans can go amiss, but taking control of your own life greatly improves the odds of success.

For the purposes of clarification two hypothetical teachers will be used as exemplars. They can only serve as the roughest guide but they can help indicate the different possibilities at different stages of your career.

The newly qualified teacher

Rachel Jones is 21 and is taking a PGCE course. Not long after starting her course (certainly by December) she has gone through the list of key points in the third box in Chapter 1 (see page 7), and has decided that she wishes to teach English or history, preferably near Sheffield; however, she is prepared to travel in order to get a school with A-level teaching. She starts reading the educational press and notices that some schools are already beginning to advertise posts in January for the following September. She also notices that in some parts of the country LEAs are putting in general advertisements for newly qualified teachers; some of them are offering attractive financial packages and help with housing.

As it does no harm to gather information, Rachel sends for details of some of these LEAs. She visits a local estate agent and asks for information about house prices just in case she decides subsequently to apply for jobs in one of these areas. She also does an Internet search (eg www.upmystreet.co.uk) to find out house prices and details of the area. She prepares her CV and starts planning the outline of a letter of application.

She starts her main teaching practice and realizes that a good reference from this school would be highly valued by prospective employers and invaluable in getting a job. She therefore makes sure that she prepares her work thoroughly, and also offers to help with extracurricular activities and attends several parent consultation evenings.

In March she sees some posts advertised in the Sheffield area that fit the parameters she has chosen. The first three applications do not produce an interview so she begins to look at schools in a wider geographical area. The nature of the normal timescale for teaching appointments – usually two weeks from the appearance of the advertisement to the closing date for applications, followed by a wait of anything up to a month for interviews – means that she cannot apply for one job at a time: she needs to have several applications in the pipeline.

She also needs to be organized: copies of letters of application should be kept with the original job details until notification that the post has been filled. Not all employers will let you know this, in which case it is better to be safe than sorry and not throw out details too soon; sometimes there can be a delay in arranging interviews for a myriad of reasons (local council elections, uncertainty about final staffing numbers, and so on). She sets up separate folders on her computer to deal with e-mail requests for details and, in cases where the school encourages e-mailed applications, copies of her letters of application.

Rachel has the advantage of not having to resign from an existing post and can therefore view the approach of 31 May without trepidation. She may, of course, be called for interview for two different jobs on the same day. In this case she needs to try to rearrange the one that is less attractive to her – not easy to decide without having seen either school. This is not always possible of course, but it is certainly worth making the enquiry. (In shortage subjects such as maths, modern foreign languages, science and technology, and certain areas of the country, good trainees are in great demand.) The end date of Rachel's time-plan is 1 September. If she has not obtained a post before then, there will always be temporary posts and possibly supply teaching, which, while not ideal for everyone, will at least afford some opportunity to teach – and to build up experience for a permanent post.

While Rachel was applying for posts teaching English or history in secondary schools, Ken Smith was also looking for his first teaching post in the Midlands. He had trained to teach primary-age children and wished to remain within travelling distance of Coventry. The timescale has been similar to Rachel's. Although constrained by geographical area, Ken knows that there are more primary schools than secondary ones, that he is not limited to one or two subjects and that he is prepared to teach children between the ages of 7 and 11. He has other preferences, including a wish to teach 'vertical' groups, which dictate the type of post he will initially apply for.

The move to middle management

After several years' teaching, Rachel and Ken may decide that they wish to apply for promotion. They refer to the second box in Chapter 1 (see page 4) to reset their career objectives before looking for a suitable post. Having decided on an action plan they then start their job search. The first box below gives examples of the type of posts available for those seeking their first promotion in primary schools and the second box gives some examples of posts available in secondary schools.

Examples of primary school posts

▌ An Early Years coordinator; two responsibility points.

▌ A senior teacher to initiate and develop the school as a focal point in the community; two responsibility points.

▌ Year 4 class teacher with responsibility for music; one responsibility point.

▌ A teacher with a special interest (eg in ICT or creative arts); one responsibility point.

▌ Coordinator for science/assessment; two responsibility points.

Examples of secondary school posts

▌ Second in English department; two responsibility points.

▌ Teacher in charge of geography; one responsibility point.

▌ Head of Year 9; one or two responsibility points available to suitable candidate.

▌ Personal programme tutor, to work with and support students with learning difficulties; one responsibility point.

▌ Assistant leader within humanities faculty; two responsibility points.

It is worth stating again that those thinking of applying for promotion should be planning at least three years ahead. They need to be able to indicate in their CVs that they have been preparing themselves for such a promotion. They should have asked for opportunities to exercise management responsibilities and should have taken part in relevant in-service training. In a secondary school suitable responsibilities could include taking a specific role within the department or becoming involved in a cross-curricular issue; in a primary school many staff find themselves taking on a particular subject (eg music) in which they become more proficient than their colleagues and contribute across several classes.

Assuming that they have already done this forward planning, our exemplars start their job search again with the third box in Chapter 1 (see page 7). Having decided on their parameters – it may be that this time Ken is willing to apply to a wider geographical area than Rachel if their circumstances have changed – they should start round about September by sorting out their CVs, planning letters of application and sending for job details. Although most appointments are still made with a starting date of September, the willingness to move in mid-year can be an advantage. It may seem an unattractive proposition to move jobs – and maybe even house – in January, but if you are prepared to do so you may gain some advantage. Only the individual can decide how important this promotion is.

An important difference between applying for promotion and going for one's first post is that the resignation dates become a major factor. This can lead to frantic activity by schools at particular times of the year: every head dreads a good member of staff getting promotion on the last day of October, which means trying to find a temporary replacement for January. If you find yourself in the position of being offered a job around about this time of the year, you need to be certain that your resignation is handed in on time. Clarify exactly how this is to be done before you go for any interview – it is another oddity of the teaching situation that resignation dates often occur in the middle of a holiday period! It is also worth noting that you should have a written offer of employment before you resign; it will usually be subject to police and medical clearance, which cannot be hurried.

While both Rachel and Ken are likely to be looking for a position with a 'responsibility' allowance, their career paths are already beginning to diverge. In primary schools there may be only one step between this promotion and a deputy headship, while in secondary schools there may well be several. It could be that Rachel will look for a post as head of department in a smaller secondary school and then look for a larger school; alternatively she may seek a second-in-department position in a large school, followed by head of department. As in the chess game referred to in the previous chapter, the possibilities become much more varied as the career plan proceeds. Secondments can be useful, provided that one does not spend too long out of the school environment. There are more opportunities available these days, relating in particular to government initiatives (eg literacy and numeracy strategies, Excellence in Cities) and to specific areas of need (eg ICT training and support).

Heading for the top

Very few people are appointed to headships without having at least some experience of deputy headship; this applies equally to primary and secondary schools. In secondary schools it is also important that you get senior management experience if at all possible before applying even for deputy headships. Few appointments are made to deputy head posts in secondary schools unless you have at least held a post with three or four responsibility points already. This can operate against teachers of subjects such as art or history, where the majority of appointments are made with two promotion points, unless there is some kind of faculty grouping. There are, of course, exceptions to this rule and some people have gained deputy headships without holding responsibility points. Such examples are not numerous, however, and can sometimes be attributed to reasons other than ability or merit.

The box below gives examples of posts in secondary schools which typically carry four or five responsibility points and which are good preparation for deputy headships. Posts for assistant headteachers are also advertised from time to time, although many are filled by internal appointments within schools.

Examples of senior posts in secondary schools

▌ Director of humanities; four responsibility points.

▌ Head of House, responsible for the pastoral and academic care of approximately 270 students; four responsibility points.

▌ Learning/resources coordinator; four responsibility points.

▌ Head of Upper School; four responsibility points.

▌ Coordinator of assessment; three or four responsibility points.

Deputy headship

It is important when applying for a deputy headship that one is clear about one's attitude to the position. While taking on a head of department post, for example, can be seen as a useful career move in itself, you need to be prepared, when applying for deputy headships, to be a deputy head or head for life, since there is often no going back to running a department from this position.

Certainly in a secondary school being a deputy head is likely to move you from being leader of a departmental team to being a junior member of the leadership team. Some people find this a problem, and it is therefore vital to make up your mind on this before applying rather than finding out to your cost that you are stuck in a position you do not like. Three to six years' experience is normally seen as the length of time in secondary deputy headship before one should apply for headship.

In a primary school there is usually only one deputy head, which indicates clearly the nature of one's level of responsibility. In some schools the post will also involve taking charge of, for example, the infants' department, finance, assessment or National Curriculum issues. Some non-contact time may be available, but this depends partly on the size of the school and partly on the philosophy of the head.

Secondary schools usually have at least two deputy heads; the employment of three or more deputy heads is uncommon nowadays. Where there is more than one deputy head, the nature of the role is less clear. Sometimes deputies are called 'first', 'second' and so on. When the head is out of school (say, for a week or longer) there is a clear legal need to know who is in charge. However, schools differ in their attitudes to how important this designation is for the rest of the time: in some places, the first deputy takes the designation very seriously, while in others all deputies carry equal status.

There are also many different approaches to the allocation of specific roles and responsibilities among deputies. It is impossible to cover the range of such roles, particularly since the patterns change from year to year. However, if you are thinking of applying for a deputy headship you need to be clear as to whether the role you are taking on is one that is an end in itself or a preparation for headship. If it is to be the latter, then you need to ensure that you have opportunities to exercise at least some of the responsibilities set out in the box below.

Essential preparation for headship

- Management of change (eg curriculum review or records of achievement).
- Control of a budget (eg capitation, INSET).
- Chairing meetings of staff from more than one department.
- Contact with governors (eg by attending at least one meeting per year).
- Change of role after two or three years.
- Some curriculum responsibility.

If you want a headship you need to clarify the most important aspects of the job: these are staffing, curriculum, finance and links with the world outside school (especially with governors). By using the box above as a checklist you should find that these are covered.

The right age?

Although things are not as rigid as they once were, it still appears to be the case that if you want to reach headship level, you need to do so before the age of 50; in fact in many cases the age limit is nearer 40 than 50 and some governing bodies actually make age a specific criterion of selection. The exception to this would be where you are going for a second headship. There also appears to be a greater reluctance to take a risk with headship appointments, which leads to a tendency to appoint staff who either work within the school's LEA or who have done so in the past. The thinking appears to be that a school can 'carry' a mistaken appointment even at deputy level but that a mistake at headship level can lead to a potentially disastrous position.

If our exemplar Rachel wants a secondary school headship she will usually be expected to have taught in at least three schools, while Ken would be expected to have taught in at least two schools as a general rule. It means that at particular times in their careers Rachel and Ken may consider a sideways move – ie to a post with no salary increase but with a different set of responsibilities, widening their experience.

3 *Applying for posts*

First step

Whether you are applying for your first post or your tenth, the general approach is the same. You first of all send for details, either by post, telephone, fax or e-mail. It is important that you read the advertiser's requirements carefully. If you are asked to send a stamped, addressed envelope, you will not get the details if you fail to do so.

It is crucial that you realize that this is the first step of the application process. Many schools keep the request for job details and therefore a scruffy letter at this stage may mean that a jaundiced view is already being taken of your suitability. (Schools like to know how many requests they receive for job details – it acts as a kind of barometer of the state of the market – and they may keep them on file to see if you subsequently apply for the post.)

If you telephone for details, you should be aware that even if the head does not receive the call personally, the person who does take it might have some influence in the initial short-listing procedure. This applies particularly at deputy head level, where your telephone manner and way of dealing with office staff are being tested even at this stage. It is wise never to underestimate the influence of the head's secretary/personal assistant in the initial sifting of applications – there is no point in being potentially brilliant at interview if your rudeness or dithering when asking for job details results in your application failing to pass the first stage.

It is now more common for schools to give an e-mail address, which allows you to request job details more quickly. If you do this, give consideration to your own e-mail address. The one you use for friends (Funkygirl or worse!) may not make the impression you want when used to request job details. Occasionally, you may be asked to send a CV at the same time as you request job details, in which case it is important that you have an up-to-date and presentable CV available. Make sure you attach the correct CV when doing this, as it is too easy to send the wrong one. Once it has gone, it is too late to recall it. The box below gives a straightforward request for job details, which can be changed as necessary.

Applying for job details

20 Any Street
Any Town
AT1 0DR
25 April 2002

Headteacher
Some School
Any Lane
Sometown
ST10 6PT

Dear Sir,
Please send me details of, and an application form for, the post of English and History at Some School.

I enclose a stamped self-addressed envelope.

Yours faithfully,
R Jones (Ms)

This letter is businesslike and to the point, which is all that you need at this stage. If the headteacher's name is given, then you should use it and sign your letter 'Yours sincerely'. If it says in the advertisement that the letter should be sent elsewhere (eg the Education Offices) or to someone else (eg the Chair of Governors), make sure you follow this instruction. If you hand-write the letter, remember to use neat and legible (not necessarily the same thing) handwriting and to date it. Be consistent in your use of punctuation and set out the letter properly; for typewritten letters you should use A4-sized paper while for handwritten requests use proper notepaper and never lined paper torn out of an exercise book. Do not forget to check the details if you use a word-processor, since applying for details for the wrong school does not go down very well.

Timetable

Closing dates are vital, which means that it may be worth considering using first-class post when requesting job details. If, however, you get your request off on a Friday night by second-class post, the school should get your letter on Monday or Tuesday; you can then have the details back by the following Friday, in time to apply over the weekend. On the other hand, you may wish to have the details more quickly to give you time to discuss them with a colleague. It is a matter for personal preference, but it is important to think the process through.

Applying for a teaching job is usually different from applying for most other jobs. In the latter, the present employer is often the last to know, days off for interview have to be disguised as holiday or sick absence, one rarely sees the other candidates, salaries are often negotiable and there is often no closing date. In teaching, on the other hand, there is a fairly standard way of filling vacancies; the box below illustrates the usual process. However, in times of shortage the usual timetable may not apply. Schools are keen to recruit the best candidates, so it may be in your interests to get your application in before the closing date.

Procedure for filling teaching vacancies

1. Post is advertised with instruction to write for details.
2. Closing date is usually two to three weeks from advertisement date.
3. Application form has to be completed.
4. A separate letter of application is usually requested.
5. Applications are not always acknowledged.
6. References are taken up.
7. Interviews are held, the result usually being announced on the same day with all the candidates present.
8. A debriefing session may be offered.

This timetable may not be adhered to in times of shortage or near the beginning of the school year.

The first point is usually fairly strictly adhered to: you may be asked to send a large stamped, addressed envelope, in which case do not send a standard-sized one. Some schools will send details in response to telephone requests, but this is more likely with headship vacancies than with others. However, it usually does no harm to telephone, unless the advertisement has very specifically indicated that only written requests for information will be accepted: things have changed during the past few years.

Closing dates are almost always given as two weeks, with exceptions more likely to occur near to 'resignation dates'. Do not expect to have your application acknowledged, although some schools do at least give a date by which they expect to have made an appointment. Once this date has passed you may assume that you have not been successful, although you should not throw out your details in case they re-advertise the post later.

It is customary to have an application form to complete, although some schools request a CV instead. In either case, a further letter of application will be expected. It is suggested that you should prepare a CV before starting your job search, since it is in any case a useful way of gathering together the information you will need to complete an application form. You need to think carefully about yourself, your career and your plans before you start applying for posts. This will make it easier to sell your qualities to someone else. Even if you do not actually use the CV for many applications, the information you have gathered together will nevertheless prove useful. The next chapter looks at this important, but neglected, area.

4 *Preparing a CV*

Any head will tell you that there are many appalling CVs; this is probably a major reason why so many schools send out application forms instead. The greatest failings with CVs are that they are too long and, quite frankly, boring; they list so many details that the important things are obscured. In this chapter we will concentrate on producing an all-purpose CV that covers no more than two sides of A4-sized paper. Guidance will be given on how to produce your own, with exemplars for teachers at different stages of their careers.

Purpose

The first thing to do is not to write but to think. What is the purpose of the CV? From your point of view it is to get you noticed; from the school's point of view it is to make an initial list of candidates who fill basic criteria. No amount of verbiage will disguise the fact that you are not qualified for a particular post, but in some cases excessive verbiage may cause such irritation that your suitability for the post may be overlooked.

It is also important to realize that your application – even for a first teaching post – may be read by six or more people. The head is the obvious first reader, but many schools automatically pass applications round the leadership team and involve at least the head of the relevant department. One or more governors may also be involved. These are all busy people and if there are 30 applications (not an unreasonable number – schools are known to get literally hundreds for some posts) they will want to be able to read them quickly. They should not have to use a highlighter pen to pick out relevant points; you should do this for them – by the way you set out your CV – and they will be grateful for it.

Basic information

The following box sets out basic information that needs to be included in a CV. The items marked with an asterisk are sometimes excluded on the grounds of equal opportunities, particularly where LEAs have very strong policies on not discriminating on the basis of race, gender or age. If this is the case you need to ensure that you follow instructions carefully: if you are asked for initials only, make sure that is all you give.

Items for inclusion in a CV

- Full name.*
- Date of birth.*
- DfES (Department for Education and Skills) reference number.
- National Insurance number.
- Address.
- Telephone number – home and work.
- Details of education and qualifications.
- Names, addresses and status of at least two referees.
- Previous teaching experience.
- Other previous experience.
- Recent courses.
- Major responsibilities exercised.
- Major recent achievements.
- Extracurricular interests.

The next box provides a layout for you to note the sort of information that you will almost always need for a CV or application form and which will not change. Additional qualifications (not just courses) can be added when necessary.

Personal details sheet

Personal details
  Full name
  Date of birth
  DfES number
  NI number

Schools attended and dates

Examinations
  (dates, subjects and grades)

University/college and dates

Qualifications
  (dates and class of degree)

It has already been suggested that a two-page CV is best. It is difficult to fit in all the required information on one page, while the case has already been made for limiting it to two pages. If you are going to use two pages, set out the CV so that it makes the most effective use of the space. One way of doing this is to include the items from the box above on the first page, which leaves page two for recent teaching experience, major responsibilities and recent courses attended; you can fit in the names of referees and extracurricular interests as appropriate. Make sure that you put your name on each page – you do not want some other candidate being given the credit for your experience if the application forms are jumbled up in the school!

While there is still some debate about whether a letter of application should be handwritten or not, it is fairly standard practice that a CV be typed or word-processed.

First application

The box below show pages one and two respectively of Rachel Jones' CV as she applies for her first teaching post. Since she has obviously not held a previous teaching post, she has more room – and more need – to amplify the experience she has gained during teaching practice, at university and in other activities. She also needs to give careful thought as to how best to set out the information over two pages.

Rachel Jones' CV, 1

First page

Rachel Jones

Personal details

Name:	Rachel Jones
Date of birth:	23 March 1980
DfES reference number:	01/12345
NI number:	AC 12 34 56 C
Address:	20 Madrid Street
	Heathtown HT1 0DR
Telephone:	(0321) 456789

Education

1984–88	Bridlane Primary School, Wessex LEA
1988–91	Field Primary School, Wessex LEA
1991–98	Meadows Comprehensive School, Northgate LEA

Examinations
1996:   GCE: English (A), English Literature (A), History (A), Mathematics (B), Technology (B), Physics (A), Biology (C), French (C), German (B)
1998:   GCE A-level: English (B), History (B), French (C)

Higher education
1998–2001   Shankly University
2001–02   Hightown University

Qualifications
2001   BA (2.1 Hons) in English and History
2002   (expected) PGCE, secondary, English with History

Second page
Rachel Jones

Teaching practice
I undertook my teaching practice at Forth School in Hightown. The school is a mixed comprehensive, 11–18. I taught the following classes:

Year 7, all-ability, English
Year 9, band three, History
Year 10, option group, GCSE History topic on the French Revolution
Year 10, band one, GCSE English Language and Literature
Year 12, GCE A-level English (Pride and Prejudice)

Major responsibilities at university
Secretary of the Students' Union, 1999–2000. Member of the editorial board of Town and Country, 1999–2001.

Other activities
I spent last summer at a holiday camp for handicapped children.

Extracurricular interests offered
I would be very willing to assist with a school magazine and to take part in visits to theatres.

Referees

Mr T Trainer	Ms I M Boss, BEd
Lecturer in Education	Headteacher
Hightown University	Forth School
Far End Avenue	Long Street
Hightown HN10 2AB	Hightown HN1 2YN

Whether Rachel uses this CV or completes an application form, the information is available in a ready-to-use form. This will make the task of organizing applications much easier.

She would be well advised to include a separate letter of application, even where this is not specified. She could also consider trying to get all the information on to one sheet; if she does this, several of the points she has included on page two could easily be part of her letter.

First steps to promotion

It may be helpful to look at how her future CV might look when she is applying for her first post as second in an English department. We can assume that she got her first post in Great School and was promoted on a temporary basis to a responsibility post while another member of staff was on a one-year secondment. She used the time to gain management experience but, realizing that she will be back to standard scale again at the end of the academic year, she decides this is the time to seek promotion elsewhere. She has been in her present post for four years. The box below illustrates her CV at this time.

Rachel Jones' CV, 2

First page

Rachel Jones

Personal details

Name:	Rachel Jones
Date of birth:	23 March 1980
DfES reference number:	01/12345
NI number:	AC 12 34 56 C
Address:	14 Broom Way
	Altcar AT1 1IR
Telephone:	(0234) 5678900

Education

1984–88	Bridlane Primary School, Wessex LEA
1988–91	Field Primary School, Wessex LEA
1991–98	Meadows Comprehensive School, Northgate LEA

Examinations passed

1996:	GCE: English (A), English Literature (A), History (A), Mathematics (B), Technology (B), Physics (A), Biology (C), French (C), German (B)
1998:	GCE A-level: English (B), History (B), French (C)

Higher education

1998–2001	Shankly University
2001–02	Hightown University

Qualifications

2001	BA (2.1 Hons) in English and History
2002	PGCE, secondary, English with History

Second page

Rachel Jones

Teaching practice
I undertook my teaching practice at Forth School in Hightown. The school is a mixed comprehensive, 11–18. I taught English and History, including GCSE and GCE A-level.

Present post
September 2002 to present: Great School (Stone LEA) Main scale + 1 resp. point (11–18 mixed comprehensive, 1,250 students).

Responsibilities
Teacher of English to GCSE and GCE A-level, with some History in the Lower School.
At present I hold a temporary 1 point allowance with responsibility for National Curriculum at Key Stage 3 within the English department; this is to cover the secondment of a member of the department.
I have also taken on responsibility during the past two years for attending GCSE moderation for oral work.

Courses

Date	Course	Length	Organizer
2003	Key Stage 3 Assessment	3 days	Stone LEA
2004	A-level Literature	1 day	New University
2005	ICT in English	3 days	Stone LEA

Extracurricular interests
I assist with the school magazine and regularly take part in visits to theatres. I spent one summer as a student at a holiday camp for handicapped children.

Referees

Mr B Grigg, BA	Ms T Reid, BEd
Headteacher	Head of English
Great School	Great School
24 West Lane	24 West Lane
Somerty SM1 6HY	Somerty SM1 6HY
Tel: 0235 1234560	0235 1234560

It can be seen that the first page has changed little. The basic information is still the same and there is no need yet to shorten it to make room for other information. Examination grades would still be expected and, of course, it will be noticed that the anticipated PGCE is now a reality.

The second page has undergone considerable change. Since Rachel has only taught in one school it might still be appropriate to include her teaching practice, although obviously this is not essential; if the information is being transferred to an application form, there is not likely to be space for this anyway. However, since there is space on the CV then it does no harm to include it. It is essential to include specific responsibilities that have been undertaken in the present post and also to have turned the offers of extracurricular help into reality – for example, the expressed willingness to help with the school magazine from her first job application. Details of courses attended are also vital and Rachel has struck a balance between furthering her professional development and being in school to do her teaching.

She has not yet undertaken further study but ought certainly to be thinking of doing so; there are many modular courses leading to certification (through the Open University and many other institutions of higher education), which allow certificates, diplomas and higher degrees to be obtained. There are also many other courses run by a myriad of providers, which although they may not be award-bearing can nevertheless be very valuable. The referees given are her present head and the head of the English department. This is fairly standard, but she could include if she wished the head of her teaching practice school or her lecturer from university. Schools sometimes only take up one reference and they certainly attach greater significance to the head's than anyone else's. She could also consider including the name of the school adviser if he or she knows Rachel.

Primary deputy headship

While Rachel has been taking on responsibilities and is now in line for promotion, Ken Smith has already moved on to a post with two responsibility points in his first post – at Armfield Primary School – and has registered for a diploma course at the local university. By 2009 he has had seven years' teaching experience and has just completed his certificate course. He decides that it is time for a move to deputy headship level and that this time he is prepared to move house to achieve that. The box below sets out his new CV.

Ken Smith's CV, 1

First page

Ken Smith
Personal details

Name:	Ken Smith
Date of birth:	2 October 1979
DfES reference number:	88/12347
NI number:	AC 12 34 57 C
Address:	54 Somme Road
	Thatchtown TT1 3IR
Telephone:	(0423) 567834

Education

1984–91	Thatchtown Primary School, Leam LEA
1991–98	Park Comprehensive School, Leam LEA

Examinations passed

1996:	GCE: English (B), English Literature (C), History (C), Mathematics (A), Technology (B), Economics (C), Chemistry (C), French (A)
1998:	GCE A-level: Mathematics (B), Economics (D), French (B)

Higher education

1998–2002	Moreton University
2006–09	McDay University (part-time, evenings)

Qualifications

2002	BEd (2.1 Hons) – secondary – specializing in Mathematics
2009	Certificate in Primary School Management

Second page
Ken Smith

Present post
September 2002 to present: Armfield Primary School, Main Scale. Thrane LEA (+ 2 resp. points 1996) (5–11 mixed, 347 pupils).

Responsibilities
I have taught Years 5 and 6, vertically grouped, since 2002. I undertook responsibility for Mathematics (including the Numeracy strategy) when I took up this post and have represented the school at cluster meetings with our local primary schools and comprehensive school during that time. We have developed effective transfer records.

In 2006 I applied for, and was appointed to, a post with responsibility within the school for assessment procedures, including the tests at the end of Key Stages 1 and 2.

Recent courses

Date	Course title	Length	Organizer
2005	ICT in Primary Schools	1 week	Thrane LEA
2006	Record-keeping	3 days	Thrane LEA
2007	Mathematics at KS3	1 day	McDay University
2008	The whole curriculum	1 week	Summer school

Extracurricular interests
I assist with games and run several school teams. I organize our summer activity week.

Referees

Ms T Rohane, BEd	Ms B Right, BA
Headteacher	Primary Adviser
Armfield Primary School	Thrane LEA
East Lane	Town Hall
Thatchtown TT2 9YT	Thatchtown TT1 1RR
Tel: 0423 5123450	Tel: 0423 5394560

Ken has only taught in one school but he has looked ahead and so is able to put down recent courses and management responsibilities that he has exercised. It is important to show that he has been involved in management of the whole school and not just of the years he has been teaching; his CV gives evidence of this. He also indicates that he was interviewed for his 'B' allowance, which shows that he got it in competition with others.

While not claiming all the credit for records, he nevertheless is right to point out that these have been developed; the use of the word 'we' shows that he has been involved and also suggests that he has worked with others, which is a necessary management skill if he wishes to get a deputy headship.

Some schools may consider that he has not had enough experience – after all, if the head is away, a deputy head will be in charge – but he is certainly right to start applying now. His willingness to move is important in widening his choice of posts and also as preparation for applying for headships in the future.

Secondary deputy headship

By 2016 Rachel has been teaching for 14 years and is now in her third post. She is thinking of applying for a deputy headship, having previously considered applying after 10 years' teaching and deciding against it. Here is how her CV might look at this time.

Rachel Jones' CV, 3

First page

Rachel Jones

Personal details

Name:	Rachel Jones
Date of birth:	23 March 1980
DfES reference number:	01/12345
NI number:	AC 12 34 56 C

Address:	35 New Road
	Old Town OT1 4TE
Telephone:	(0123) 789045

Education
1984–88	Bridlane Primary School, Wessex LEA
1998–91	Field Primary School, Wessex LEA
1991–98	Meadows Comprehensive School, Northgate LEA

Examinations passed
1996:	9 GCE O-levels
1998:	3 GCE A-levels

Higher education
1998–01	Shankly University
2001–02	Hightown University (part-time)
2013–15	Oldfield University (part-time)

Qualifications
2001	BA (2.1 Hons) in English and History
2002	PGCE, secondary, English with History
2015	Diploma in Educational Management

Referees
Ms G Brown	Mr B Brough
Headteacher	Senior Adviser
Fir School	Wood LEA
Great Wood Road	Leafy Lane
Forest Town FR4 3RE	Forest Town FR1 6TR
Tel: 0350 235670	Tel: 0350 3425470

Second page
Rachel Jones

Present post
September 2012 to present: Fir School (Wood LEA) Main Scale
+ 4 resp. points (11–18 mixed comprehensive, 945 students)

Previous posts

September 2007 – August 2012:	Leafy School (Stone LEA) Main Scale + 2 resp. points (11–18 mixed comprehensive, 1,050 students)
September 2002 – August 2007:	Great School (Stone LEA) Main Scale + 1 resp. point (11–18 mixed comprehensive, 1,250 students)

Major responsibilities

2005	Great School	GCSE moderation
2006	Great School	Key Stage English (temp 1 resp. point)
2007	Leafy School	Second in English department
2011	Leafy School	Acting head of department
2012	Fir School	Head of English department
2014	Fir School	Chair of heads department
	Fir School	Chair of appraisal committee
2015	Fir School	Member of finance committee

Recent courses

Date	Course title	Length	Organizer
2011	Head of department	1 week	Cedar University
2013	Appraisal techniques	3 days	Wood LEA
2014	Making the team work	4 days	ICH plc
2015	(Diploma in Management – see first page)		

Extracurricular interests
I am responsible for the community newsletter, which goes out to parents and others in the community every month. I also regularly organize theatre visits.

You will notice that page one has been changed and that the referees have been added to it, with the other items being spaced more closely together. The basic information is still there but doing this leaves more room on the second page to highlight important responsibilities exercised and courses attended. Not every course is listed, since Rachel does not wish to give the impression that she is never in school! However, the courses she has listed indicate that she is preparing herself to take on the wider school responsibilities that are expected from a deputy head. She also mentions the diploma again, in case it is overlooked by some of those involved in the appointment.

She does not labour the point about the range of classes she has taught since it will be assumed that if she has been teaching for 14 years in schools with sixth forms, and is now a head of department, she will have experience across the age and ability range. Her experience in three schools has given her a breadth of knowledge that will be helpful in answering questions if she gets to interview.

At this level she knows that she must be prepared to move for promotion; in fact, not moving may prove a handicap if she later decides to apply for a headship. She could consider a move to an assistant head in a different school; however, she is now 36 and might need to move again in three years' time for a deputy headship. It is important that she considers this move carefully and is selective about the posts she applies for. If she is not happy about the atmosphere in any school she goes to, she would be well advised to withdraw. As indicated earlier in the book, a good school for her purposes is not necessarily the same as a good school in the eyes of parents: it is a school where she will be given a level of responsibility commensurate with her status and which allows her to prepare herself for headship. If she later decides not to go for a headship, nothing is lost.

Headship

Before applying for a headship, both Rachel and Ken may decide to take the opportunity of a secondment. These opportunities can last from a term to a year (or even longer). If the secondment lasts longer than a year, it may be difficult to return to one's existing school. Indeed, some schools may not agree to a longish secondment. Fixed-term posts are now more common – the disadvantage is that there is no guarantee of a job at the end.

The final examples of CVs are when Rachel and Ken are applying for headships. The first box below shows Ken's when he decides to apply for his headship in 2015 (at the age of 35), while the next box is Rachel's when she decides to apply for hers in 2020 (at the age of 40). It is worth noting that Rachel could in some circumstances be earning more as a deputy head than Ken will be as a head. This is due partly to the fact that primary schools are usually smaller than secondary schools and partly to the fact that older children are often worth more per head when money is allocated to schools.

Ken Smith's CV, 2

First page

Ken Smith

Personal details

Name:	Ken Smith
Date of birth:	2 October 1979
DfES reference number:	92/12347
NI number:	AC 12 34 57 C
Address:	48 Cedar Drive
	Idyll ID2 8HC
Telephone:	(0677) 345678

Education

1984–91	Thatchtown Primary School, Leam LEA
1991–98	Park Comprehensive School, Leam LEA

Examinations passed
1996:   8 GCE O-levels
1998:   3 GCE A-levels

Higher education
1998–02   Moreton University
2006–09   McDay University (part-time, evenings)
2013–15   McDay University (part-time, evenings)

Qualifications
2002   BEd (2.1 Hons) – secondary – specializing in
           Mathematics
2009   Certificate in Primary School Management.
           Diploma in School Management Studies
2015   NPQH

Referees
Mr R Holmes, BA, MEd   Ms B Fulton, BEd
Headteacher   Chief adviser
Hazel Primary School   Little LEA
Fast lane   Town Hall
Down Town DT3 5RF   Down Town DT1 9UT
Tel: 0221 3423450   Tel: 0221 4594560

Second page
Ken Smith

Present post
September 2010 to present: Hazel Primary School, Deputy Head
2010, 5–11 mixed, 435 pupils (Little LEA)

Previous post
September 2002–August 2010: Armfield Primary School, Main
Scale, 5–11 mixed, 347 pupils (2 resp. points, 2006)

Major responsibilities
I have taught Years 5 and 6, vertically grouped, since 2002.
2002   Armfield Primary School   Coordinator of mathematics
       Armfield Primary School   Cluster representative
2006   Armfield Primary School   Assessment procedures, inc.
                                  KS1 and KS2 tests

2009	Armfield Primary School	One term acting deputy head to cover a secondment
2010	Hazel Primary School	Deputy head, inc. supply cover + resp. for capitation
2003	Hazel Primary School	Member of governing body (inc. curriculum committee)

Recent courses

Date	Course title	Length	Organizer
2008	The whole curriculum	1 week	Summer school
2009	Assessment 2000	3 days	Leam LEA
2011	Planning school review	2 days	HUP plc
2013	Team building	4 days	Leam LEA
2014	Leadership styles	1 week	Summer school
2015	Deputy head induction*	3 days	Little LEA

*I was a contributor to this course, at the invitation of the Chief Adviser.

Extracurricular interests
I assist with games and run several school teams. I am responsible for school camp, which is run every year for all Year 6 pupils.

Rachel Jones' CV, 4

First page
Rachel Jones

Personal details

Name:	Rachel Jones
Date of birth:	23 March 1980
DfES reference number:	01/12345
NI number:	AC 12 34 56 C
Address:	35 Far Avenue
	Old Town OT11 4IH

Telephone: (0123) 1237890

Education

1984–88	Bridlane Primary School, Wessex LEA
1998–91	Field Primary School, Wessex LEA
1991–98	Meadows Comprehensive School, Northgate LEA

Examinations passed

1996	9 GCE O-levels
1998	3 GCE A-levels

Higher education

1998–01	Shankly University
2001–02	Hightown University
2013–17	Oldfield University (part-time)

Qualifications

2001	BA (2.1 Hons) in English and History
2002	PGCE, secondary, English with History
2015	Diploma in Educational Management
2017	MEd (Educational Management)
2018	NPQH

Referees

Mr B Jones	Mr A Gorman
Headteacher	Senior Adviser
Acacia School	Track LEA
Acacia Avenue	Centre Lane
Only Town ON4 4TR	Only Town ON1 3DE
Tel: 0334 2325670	Tel: 0334 5625470

Second page
Rachel Jones

Present post
September 2006 to present: Acacia School (Track LEA). Deputy headteacher, 11–18 mixed comprehensive, 980 students.

Previous posts
September 2012–2016   Fir School (Wood LEA). Upper Scale + 4 resp. points, 11–18 mixed comprehensive, 945 students
September 2007–August 2012   Leafy School (Stone LEA). Main Scale + 2 resp. points, 11–18 mixed comprehensive, 1,050 students

September 2002–August 2007   Great School (Stone LEA)
Main Scale + 1 resp. point, 11–18 mixed comprehensive,
1,250 students

Major responsibilities

2006	Great School	Key Stage 3 (temp 1 resp. point)
2007	Leafy School	Second in English department
2011	Leafy School	Acting head of department
2012	Fir School	Head of English department
2014	Fir School	Chair of heads of department
		Chair of appraisal committee
2015	Fir School	Member of finance committee
2016	Acacia School	Deputy Headteacher (curriculum and staffing)
2017	Acacia School	Chair of capitation committee
2018	Acacia School	Attended governors' meetings

Recent courses

Date	Course title	Length	Organizer
2014	Making the team work	4 days	ICH plc
2016	Leadership roles	3 days	Track LEA
2017	Appraisal review	2 days	Track LEA
2018	Governing schools	3 days	ICH plc
2019	Motivating staff*	4 days	A University
	Managing change	1 week	Summer school

*I contributed to this course.

Extracurricular interests
I am particularly interested in publications and take responsibility for liaison with the media. I also organize the annual summer camp for all Year 9 students.

I have had several articles published in School Management Today, the monthly journal for school heads and deputies.

You will notice that both Rachel and Ken have contributed to courses as well as attending them; Rachel has also had some articles published. These activities alone will not guarantee an interview, never mind a job, but at least they indicate something to set both of them apart from other applicants. Some responsibilities (except those for which an allowance was given) from earlier in their careers have been omitted, as have some courses.

As indicated at the end of Chapter 3, you may not need to send the CV; however, by preparing it you are psychologically geared up to applying for posts and you have the information readily available for completing application forms. In either case, the objective must be to get an interview. To do this you need first to write a letter of application. The next chapter deals with this key step.

5 *Getting an interview*

By now you are organized: you have written your CV and you have sent for details of some posts that interest you. The vast majority of posts at all levels in the profession still ask for an application form to be completed. Although an application letter is not always requested, it is usually assumed that one will be sent.

Application form

Application forms are not necessarily user-friendly; most are likely to be specifically designed for those applying for teaching posts but in some areas of the country there is one application form for all prospective employees of the local authority. There are no absolute rules about filling in application forms; in some cases the school is very keen that the form is completed in detail, while others send out the form simply because it happens to be there. In these uncertain circumstances, it is better to be safe than sorry. The box below sets out guidelines that should be helpful.

Notes on completing application forms

- Unless stated otherwise, fill in all sections of the form in as much detail as possible.
- Complete the form carefully in black ink. (It is worth experimenting with a few pens to find one which helps you write neatly and quickly, but note that many application forms are printed on porous paper which will smudge any ink used; ball-point is probably safer.)

▌ Note such details as whether you are asked for your surname (or family name) first or last.

▌ Sign and date the form.

▌ Note carefully where and by when it should be returned. If there are any uncertainties – and make sure that they are not just your failure to read the details carefully – it does no harm to make a telephone enquiry. Remember that when you do, you should consider yourself to be already at interview and act accordingly.

▌ If you are copying the information from your prepared CV, you do not need to keep a separate copy; however, if you are asked for any information which is not on your CV, it is important to keep a copy of your answer in case you are called for interview.

▌ If the space for a letter of application or list of recent courses is hopelessly inadequate, indicate that you are attaching separate details; then make sure that you do!

▌ Do not send a CV as well as the completed application form. (Do not send it *instead of* the form either; some job details will include a very firm injunction about this, but even where they do not, you are taking a great risk by ignoring the form.)

▌ Remember that this may be the fiftieth form you have completed, but it is the first knowledge the selectors have of your interest in their job. They will not make allowances for tiredness or boredom on your part.

So far, you have been establishing that you have the basic qualifications for the post for which you are applying. In these early stages – sending for the details, making telephone enquiries, completing the application form or sending your CV – you are trying to make sure that you stay in the race. It would be unusual indeed for someone to get a job on the basis of these first steps but it is not exceptional for someone to inadvertently put themselves out of the running by lack of attention to some detail or other.

Selection criteria

It is important to know that many interviewing committees use detailed job and person specifications to do the initial sorting of applications. They may have criteria, listed under 'essential' and 'desirable'. Such criteria could include length of teaching experience, age, number of schools in which you have taught, knowledge and/or experience of, for example, multi-racial, mixed, comprehensive or grammar schools.

If you have not seen these criteria – only some schools send them out with job details – then you do not know whether you lack some of the basic qualifications for that particular post. There is not much you can do about this: if you lack some experience which the committee deem to be 'essential', then you are not likely to be interviewed, but do not be put off applying if you lack one or two of the 'desirable' ones.

References and referees

Few things are more misunderstood by applicants for teaching posts than the business of 'taking up references'. It is a mistake to assume that because you have had your references taken up it is necessarily a good sign: it may just mean that a large number of, or even all, references are being taken up as a matter of policy. I have even heard one head suggest that taking up a particular candidate's reference might 'encourage him', even though there was no intention of calling him for interview!

If there is a pattern, it would appear to be that schools are most likely to take up the head's reference for applicants for standard scale posts, and those with one or two responsibility points, only if they are seriously considering the person's application. One reason for this is that the tradition of schools sending a stamped, addressed envelope to referees can be an expensive business. If the school has had only a dozen applications they may decide to take up references from everyone's first referee; it is certainly the case that the second reference is taken up with less frequency.

When it comes to posts on higher scales, and particularly at senior management level (assistant or deputy head), it is more likely that having one's references taken up is a sign of at least some interest.

For headship applications there was a tradition of schools under LEA control taking up an LEA reference. Governors are now responsible for the appointment of headteachers, advised by the LEA. The influence of the LEA over the governors varies from one area to the next, and indeed from one school to the next. This means that before applying for a headship you should ensure that your LEA adviser who will respond to this request knows who you are – not always the case in a large LEA – and can write about you. Many headships are filled without any reference at all to your present head or any of your other named referees. Be warned, however, that at least one LEA traditionally took up a reference on every applicant for a headship. In this case having a reference taken up did not give any clue as to perceived suitability for the post.

Many governing bodies feel very confident in appointing a headteacher, while others do not. It is probably the single most important action they take and increasingly some are turning to consultants to help with the process. This consultancy can take the form of advising the governors on how to go about the appointment process and possibly helping with the mechanics of it. However, in some cases the main initial work may be handed over to a firm of professional recruitment consultants.

The best general advice is to assume an interview is in the offing only when one receives a letter or a telephone call. One teacher I know was told by her head that he had just received a telephone call asking for her to attend for interview at 10 am the following Friday. It is a sign of the times that she faxed her confirmation.

There is some unfairness in the system of references in that failure to put one's present head as first referee could be viewed with suspicion; if you do not get on with your present head, you may feel that you will have difficulty in getting another post.

Your safeguard against this is to use the performance management system of the school in a positive way, ensure that your head knows in advance that you are applying for other posts and try to negotiate the areas that the reference will cover. Most heads these days are ready to ensure that references they write deal with facts; it is in their interests to ensure that they do not give staff cause for grievance, since it is not unusual for selection committees to let candidates know what was written about them. If this turns out to be inaccurate or damning, the likelihood is that the head will have a very dissatisfied member of staff to deal with on his or her return to school.

Testimonials are not usually seen as worthy of much consideration by any selection committee; I have yet to meet anyone who could show me a testimonial that was other than glowing! Many schools actually enjoin applicants not to send testimonials and this seems to be good advice.

Letters of application

It remains the case that the most important thing in determining whether you get an interview is your letter of application. This differs from what we have talked about so far in that a good letter can make a positive difference in your job search, whereas the application form or CV is more likely to have a negative effect if not properly prepared. Some general advice will be given on writing the letter and then examples will be given, with the caveat that ultimately they cannot be a substitute for your own thinking. Copying them from this book could be disastrous if the head or someone else on the appointments committee has read it too!

Purposes of letters of application

There are two interested parties here: the first (the applicant) wants to interest the second (the selector) in granting an interview. The letter is doubly important both in selecting for an interview and also in making the final selection if there is any doubt after the interview. It is not unusual for a selection committee to review the written applications of some or all candidates in the event of them having difficulty in reaching a decision. The following box sets out some questions to think about before you sit down to write any letter of application.

Questions to answer before writing letters of application

▌ Have I read the job details carefully? Can I begin to picture what the school wants in its ideal appointment?

▌ What *exactly* is the school looking for?

▌ Do I really believe I want this job?

▌ What are my strengths from the school's point of view?

▌ How can I convince the school that I should be interviewed?

▌ Have I checked the school's OFSTED reports?

▌ Have I looked at the school's Web site?

If you do not read the details carefully you may make basic errors in your letter, which will rule you out of the appointment committee's consideration. Some schools send only sketchy information, but anything they do send needs to be read very carefully. You can then try to build up a picture of the school, and in particular the department where you may be working if the post is below deputy head level or, if it is at deputy head level, the way the senior management team operates. At headship level your dealings with the governors will be crucial so you need to judge what kind of head they are looking for – remember Churchill, who was seen as the ideal man for the job in wartime but not in peacetime, when different strengths were called for.

Having studied the details and built up your mental image, you have then got to believe that you really want the job, on the grounds that if you are not convinced then it will be hard to convince someone else.

If you decide that you do want the job, then it is time to be positive about what you can offer. You need to strike a balance between over-confidence and self-effacement: if you do not list your strengths you can be sure that no one else will.

Pen or word-processor?

Your letter can be typed/word-processed or handwritten. The arguments against word-processing are that it is too easy to run off a standard letter without tailoring it to your audience; however, most people who write applications by hand must also start with some kind of template, if only in their heads. At least one LEA insists that letters of application for headship should be handwritten, but most job details will not include an injunction either way. Personally I find that even neat handwriting is not necessarily very easy to read.

I think that most selection committees will accept a letter that has been either neatly handwritten (in black, for easy photo-copying) or typed/word-processed. Two points that may be worth making are that a word-processed letter can look awful if it is not set out neatly and that spelling mistakes are less easily disguised. If you do use a word-processor it is sometimes more difficult to tailor your letter exactly to the needs of a particular post, so it is extremely important to check it thoroughly. Equally, if you write your letter by hand, avoid striking out mistakes or covering them in correction fluid. Rewrite the letter instead. Use decent paper, preferably A4-sized. The next box gives some suggestions on how to set out your letter logically.

Hints on setting out a letter of application

▌ Outline briefly but succinctly your experience as it relates to the post.

▌ Highlight relevant achievements.

▌ Indicate what motivates you to teach and what you would hope to achieve in the post.

▌ Set out some ideas on how you would tackle the job.

▌ Indicate how you have prepared yourself for promotion.

▌ Finish on a positive note (the sample letters indicate some suitable endings).

▌ Aim to write not more than two sides of typed A4 paper – or the equivalent number of words if handwritten; an exception to this might be at headship level, where you should not exceed three sides. (Going on too long sounds like desperation and will talk you out of an interview more quickly than talking you into one.)

It cannot be emphasized too strongly that your letter of application needs to reflect your own views. Every letter reveals something about its writer – either consciously or subconsciously – and the thesis of this book is that in the final analysis you should be looking for a post in which your strengths will be valuable. Thus the general advice in the box above and the examples of letters which follow in this chapter need to be modified to suit your own needs. For example, there may be times – this is especially so at headship level – when it is more important to start off with your educational philosophy than with a list of your achievements, since many of the applicants will have a similar list of achievements to produce. There is more importance attached to an applicant's personality and management style than one might think.

A practice which can be helpful is to send a short covering letter in addition to your main letter of application: this allows you to fit more into your two or three pages, which becomes particularly important as your career develops. It also allows you to use your own personalized notepaper, if you have any.

Some examples

Below is an example of a covering letter that might be written by Rachel Jones when applying for her first teaching post. Such a letter will not differ greatly whether applying for a first teaching post or for a headship, so only one example will be given. This is followed by Rachel's letter of application.

Example of a covering letter

20 Madrid Street
Heathtown
_HT1 0DR_
3 June 2002

Mr O Redding
Headteacher
The Brilliant School
Sunset Road
LOVELYPOOL LO2 5TY

Dear Mr Redding,

I wish to apply for the post of English teacher (Standard Scale) at The Brilliant School.

I attach my completed application form and a separate letter, setting out of my experience on teaching practice, my personal philosophy of teaching English, and information about my extracurricular interests.

Yours sincerely,
Rachel Jones

Rachel Jones – letter of application for a first post

I have pleasure in applying for the post of English teacher at The Brilliant School. I graduated with a BA (2.1 Honours) degree in English and History from Shankly University in 2001. At present I am taking my PGCE at Hightown University.

My teaching practice was spent at Forth School (Hightown), where I taught English in Years 7, 10 and 12 and History in Years 9 and 10. My English teaching included GCE A-level work and I was also involved in teaching GCSE in both English and History.

Before embarking on my PGCE year I undertook three weeks' observation at our local comprehensive school so that I could see what teaching would involve. During that time I assisted several of the staff with their lessons and was very impressed by the achievement shown by the pupils.

It was this experience as much as anything which inspired me to enter the teaching profession. I believe that literacy skills are vital in the present-day world and also that young people have much to learn from literature. I would therefore wish to encourage young people to develop wide experience of reading.

During my time on teaching practice I gave some help to the member of staff responsible for the school magazine and spent some time in the library. The school is making use of books and of newer forms of technology (including interactive teaching materials), both of which are, in my view, very important.

My extracurricular interests include reading, photography and badminton. I have some proficiency in the clarinet and would be willing to contribute to the school's musical activities. At university I worked on the fortnightly newspaper. I would like to work at The Brilliant School and would welcome the opportunity to discuss my views at interview.

Yours sincerely,

Rachel Jones

For this first post there is not very much detail in the main letter, so it might be better to combine it with the covering letter. It will depend on whether you write or type it and how it looks in practice. Layout can make a difference – a point worth reiterating.

Although this letter may look a little brief, it should be remembered that there is already a lot of detail on the application form and the only part repeated here draws attention to experience and interests. It might even be possible, depending on the layout of the application form, to include the letter there. Remember these are only guidelines, not absolute rules.

When going for a second post, of course, Rachel has much more experience to call on and can write more. Below is a possible letter of application for a post as a second in department, which is her next step towards a head of department post.

Rachel Jones – letter of application for a second-in-department post

I have been teaching English for five years, across the age and ability range, at Great School; this has included teaching to GCSE and GCE A-level. The students I teach consistently obtain high grades in English at both examination levels. I attend the examination board meetings to moderate GCSE oral marks and organize their moderation within school. My timetable has also included classes in the lower school and I am conversant with the requirements of Key Stage 3 of the National Curriculum.

I held a temporary post with responsibility for Key Stage 3 during the secondment of another member of the department. I am one of a team of staff who contribute to the teaching of Drama in Year 7.

The temporary post that I held offered me the opportunity to develop my management skills, working with all the staff to coordinate our lower school teaching. This also involved meeting with representatives of other departments to ensure a whole-school approach to our teaching and assessment policies where appropriate. I feel that my organizational skills were useful in this post and I learnt a considerable amount about managing a key part of the department's work.

We have been developing our use of information technology and have several networked computers in use in the department. I use

---

a computer at home and am comfortable using standard 'Office' packages. Many of my teaching materials are stored on the school network, from where they can be easily retrieved for both class and individual student work.

In addition to my teaching commitments, I assist with the school magazine, working with a group of very enthusiastic students. We run regular visits, some of which I also organize.

I enjoy teaching and seeing students achieve their potential, both socially and academically. I am convinced that English has a vital contribution to make to our students' lives, both during adolescence and as they become adults. I believe that students must be equipped with high-level communication skills and a love for literature, and see both objectives as mutually supportive. During my first five years of teaching I have learnt a lot, about the organization of learning within the classroom and about how an effective department is run. My temporary post has allowed me the opportunity to take on management responsibilities, which I enjoyed. I feel that I am ready for promotion and would see the post at Leafy School as offering the scope to continue my career development.

I would welcome the opportunity of an interview to discuss these points in greater detail.

Yours sincerely,

Rachel Jones

A major fault when writing letters of application is to write either too much or not enough; I suspect that the former is more common than the latter, although there are some amazingly short letters sent in from time to time. In Rachel's letter she has tried to steer a middle course between the two extremes. She has highlighted the range of her teaching, and has very sensibly stressed her examination work. If her students do get good grades she should mention this – a letter of application is not the place to have self-doubts or to be diffident.

It is important to establish her standing as a classroom teacher, since that will be the main part of her job. However, she is also looking for a post with some management responsibility, and therefore must spend some time indicating her management skills. Notice that she uses the mention of the temporary post both to emphasize her experience and to suggest that she has good organizational ability; the appointments panel can further explore this through her references and at interview if she is called. The kind of responsibility she has been exercising is not untypical of that expected of the holder of two responsibility points in a large department.

Her extracurricular activities are indicated and she uses this to point out that she can enthuse students; note that she is quite subtle about this in that she suggests the students are enthusiastic – she will get the credit by association. The fact that she mentions enthusiasm also says something about her in itself: remember the point about one's use of language revealing a lot? The letter finishes positively, asserting why Rachel teaches and summarizing why she is ready for promotion.

We assume that she gets this post and that by the year 2012 she is applying for a post as head of department. Here is a letter that she might write at that time.

Rachel Jones – letter of application for a head of department post

I have been teaching English for 10 years, across the age and ability range; this has included teaching to GCSE and GCE A-level. The students I teach consistently obtain high grades in English at both examination levels. I have also considerable experience of Key Stage 3 teaching and assessment, having held specific responsibility for this in two schools.

Recently I have been acting as head of department to cover a maternity leave. This has given me invaluable experience in managing a department and has convinced me that I have reached a point in my career where I am ready for promotion to such a post.

We have undertaken several important initiatives at Leafy School during my time there. One particular development with which I have been closely associated is the use of post-16 students in a 'paired reading' scheme. Before students start work on this

---

scheme they are given specific training. The way the scheme operates is that all Year 7 children who have reading difficulties are assigned a post-16 student to work with them on a daily basis. There have been enormous improvements in reading levels as a result of this scheme and it has been the subject of a feature in the Times Educational Supplement.

We have also developed our use of information technology and every English room has its own computers, used mainly for drafting work and producing collaborative magazines. We are very involved in the management of the Resources Centre and use the ICT network regularly, particularly for analysing newspaper styles and for making close textual study of works such as Hamlet.

In addition to my teaching commitments, I assist with the school magazine, working with a group of very enthusiastic students. We run regular theatre visits, some of which I also organize.

I enjoy teaching and seeing students achieve their potential academically and socially. I am convinced that English has a vital contribution to make to our students' lives, both during adolescence and as they become adults. I believe that students must be equipped with high-level communication skills and a love for literature, and see both objectives as mutually supportive.

I am convinced that a successful school is possible only when heads of department function effectively. The key element in doing this is staff management, so that everyone feels fully involved in, and committed to, the policies of the department. As second in department I have taken on specific responsibility for lower school English; I regularly chair departmental meetings and feel that I balance the need for listening with the need for action. During this period I have sought to give other staff similar experience by encouraging them to chair departmental meetings. I recently attended a very useful course for heads of department, at Cedar University.

I feel that I am ready for promotion and would see the post at Fir School as offering the scope to continue my career development. I would welcome the opportunity of an interview to discuss my application in greater detail.

Yours sincerely,

Rachel Jones

Some parts of this letter are recognizable from her earlier one – she still gives the same reasons for enjoying teaching – but obviously she now has more experience on which to draw. She mentions in particular the paired reading scheme; she has introduced this to the school, a fact which will become even clearer if the head mentions it in her reference and at interview if the panel ask about it. However, she uses the word 'we', partly to try to avoid the over-use of 'I' and partly to indicate that she works well as part of a team.

She has had a further stroke of luck – another acting post! – but equally importantly she has been preparing for this promotion and has attended relevant courses. She attended a head of department course as soon as she got the acting post so that she could make full use of this particular circumstance; this shows the value of being prepared for whatever strokes of good luck happen to appear. The course will be listed on her application but again she highlights it. She also indicates her management style by pointing out that she has allowed others to chair departmental meetings.

One thing that is not included here is specific mention of Fir School. If Rachel is aware of any particular qualities that they want, such as enthusiasm, then she should try to indicate activities demonstrating this quality. (The way she did it in her previous letter, for example, was more effective than simply asserting, 'I am enthusiastic'.) A short paragraph should be included near the end of the letter, if you have been given specific details about the school or if you have researched information about the school (for example, via its Web site).

For the next example we look at Ken's letter of application for the deputy headship of Hazel Primary School, the post which he took up in September 2010. Now that Ken is applying for a position which can leave him in charge of the school during the head's absence – and for longer if the head happens to be taken ill – he needs to show that he has the experience and confidence to run the school. His temporary post is fortuitous, but his attendance at relevant courses is not because now he is ready to take advantage of the opportunities that come his way.

Ken Smith – letter of application for deputy headship

I wish to apply for the post of Deputy Headteacher of Hazel Primary School. I have eight years' teaching experience and have held two responsibility points in my present position at Armfield Primary School for the past four years. Armfield is a 5–11 mixed school with 347 pupils on roll.

We operate vertical grouping, with age ranges of 5–7, 7–9 and 9–11, which is similar to that operated at Hazel Primary School. We have gradually developed our techniques to maximize the benefits which such a form of organization can bring, particularly with regard to carrying out the SATs at the end of each Key Stage. I teach the older children, although I spend on average one day per week in the other two age groupings in order to be familiar with the needs and developments throughout the school.

When I started my teaching career at Armfield I took on particular responsibility for Mathematics (including the numeracy strategy), keeping staff up to date with the requirements of the National Curriculum in programmes of study and assessment. I represented the school at meetings with our colleagues in the local comprehensive school in order to secure continuity between the two phases of education.

When the teacher responsible for assessment procedures throughout the school, including KS1 and KS2 tests, was promoted in 2006, I was appointed to the post, which carried two responsibility points. During this past year I have been acting deputy and had to cover a member of staff on secondment; from time to time I act for the head in her absence.

I attend suitable courses, the two most significant recent ones being a summer school on 'The Whole Curriculum' and a three-day course on 'Assessment'.

I chair the staff meetings which are called regularly to plan the implementation of assessment and I also take charge of the group looking at the development of economic and industrial understanding with our older children. All staff at Armfield contribute to our programme of extracurricular activities, my part in this being on the sports side, running several teams of both boys and girls.

With my experience to date – and particularly my present temporary post – I feel that I am ready to take on a deputy headship. At Armfield School I have had regular contact with parents and governors, which has led to very productive partnerships in the interests of the children.

My personal philosophy of education is based on ensuring that every child not only is given a thorough grounding in the basics of literacy and numeracy, but also is excited by the possibilities opened up by a rich and varied curriculum. I feel that I would fit in very naturally with the philosophy of Hazel School as set out in the information provided and would welcome the opportunity to expand on my views at interview.

Yours sincerely,

Ken Smith

He makes specific reference to vertical grouping, which has obviously been mentioned in the job details, and also shows that he is aware of the advantages of the system. He does not, however, ignore the fact that such a system needs care and thought to make it work effectively.

When setting out his personal philosophy he emphasizes the importance of literacy and numeracy – which is particularly relevant bearing in mind that some of the readers of his application will almost certainly be parent-governors – but also suggests that their development is not incompatible with an imaginative approach to the curriculum. He mentions the links with the secondary school, which indicates that he can take on responsibilities outside the school. As with the other examples given, this should not be seen as a model approach, merely as one way of writing a letter of application.

Rachel's application for a secondary deputy headship will deal with a different type of school but will nevertheless highlight her experience, put forward her own philosophy and give specific examples of how she has gained senior management experience. This will make the point that she has some knowledge of what senior management in a secondary school means in practice.

The move to headship is quite rightly seen as different from all the others, because no matter how much team management is practised in an institution – whether a small primary school or a large secondary one – ultimately the buck stops with the head. There is also enough research evidence available to suggest that the quality of the head makes a very significant difference to the success of the school. This makes the decision to appoint a head the most important one that any governing body will make.

As if this were not enough, it is useful to reflect that this is the appointment where the governors will not have the current head's active involvement in the process. For other posts the head will organize the advertising, the job details, the visits to the school and the structure of the interview, while checking that the governors are happy with the way it is done; for the appointment of the head's successor a lot of responsibility will fall on the chair of governors. For LEA schools the governors will have advice available from the Chief Education Officer – whether they want it or not – but the final decision on how and who to appoint will be theirs.

The application

You might well ask at this point how this makes a difference to the applicant. Below are listed some of the more important ways in which applying for a headship differs from any other job in the school.

Notes for applicants for headship

▌ Your personality will be more significant than with any other post: how you approach the job – both in terms of your educational philosophy and your management style – will be crucial to the success of the school.

- You must be willing to make the final decision when called upon to do so.
- Your job will involve far more dealings with the other contributors to the school (governors, parents, LEA, community, etc) than you are likely to have had in the past.
- You will achieve most of what you want to do through other adults, not through your own interventions in the classroom. Headship requires skills at managing the efforts of adults as opposed to those of children; there are significant differences!
- The value of your teaching in the past will lie in giving you a deeper understanding of the main business of the school, not in exercising the classroom skills and techniques you have acquired; many heads, even in primary schools, teach little or not at all.
- Your working day will be different, particularly at lunchtimes; while other teaching staff can confine their work to the morning and afternoon sessions, you cannot. Your job has no specific time limits, either in the number of hours per day or days per year. (While it is true that most teachers do not limit themselves to being in school on only 195 days a year, they can at least choose to do so if they wish.)
- You will be responsible for the work of other staff such as caretakers, technicians, secretaries and so on. Personnel management will have a wider scope than it did previously.
- You will be called upon to give the lead in setting – and delivering – the 'vision' of the school.

These points are not intended to put you off – most heads will tell you that they have never had such a satisfying job in their lives, but the ones who do not enjoy the post must lead extremely unpleasant lives indeed. Rather the points are designed to assist you in deciding whether or not headship is for you. If you decide that it is, then you need to be aware that all the points mentioned will lead to some significant differences in the way the appointment will be made; here are the most important.

Differences in making headship appointments

▌ More attention needs to be paid to your philosophy of education in your application. Although it sounds a little surprising, you are not likely to be questioned deeply on your ability in the classroom.

▌ There will be greater involvement of governors in the process, and you are likely to be interviewed by a panel of up to 20 people.

▌ It is more important for your educational philosophy to accord with that of the governors than for any other appointment. Trying to be other than yourself – just to get the job – is even more disastrous at this level.

▌ Selection methods will vary greatly. Methods of appointment to other posts are more likely to fall into a set pattern than are those for headships. (More will be said about this later.)

▌ There may be a tendency to 'play safe', which means that appointments may be made from candidates from the school's LEA. However, there are exceptions to every rule.

▌ The appearance of a national advertisement for most posts indicates a wish to recruit from as wide a field as possible. For headship (and deputy headship) appointments, LEA schools are required to advertise nationally; they are not, however, required to appoint from outside the locality. The problem for applicants is that it is not easy to tell which posts are 'open' and which are not.

Let us suppose that Rachel is now a deputy head and has decided she does in fact wish to apply for a headship. Her letter of application needs to set out clearly her experience and educational philosophy, while at the same time conveying some idea of her personality. The short-listing panel will almost certainly have produced written criteria to guide them. Such criteria could include length of teaching experience, experience at senior management level, age, qualifications and evidence of attendance at management courses. Additional criteria might include recent experience in particular types of school (for example, 11–18, inner-city, suburban, selective, comprehensive, multi-racial, voluntary-aided, mixed/single-sex).

One can assume that most of this information will be gleaned from the application forms and/or the CVs. Once you have passed this initial filtering process, it is your letter of application that will show whether you stand out as the kind of person they are looking for. Given this, I feel that you should start your letter with your personality and educational philosophy, followed by details of relevant experience.

It is critical that you read all the information that has been sent to you: this can vary from two sheets of A4 paper to a folder full of information. Do not assume, incidentally, that the information sent will necessarily give a clue as to whether the governors are genuinely seeking applicants from all over the country or indeed that it will even reflect the quality of the school. Another point worth making is that you should not expect there to be any obvious rationale that will help you decide which posts offer the best chance of getting an interview. It is often said by those who have been successful that applying for a headship is a form of lottery, which suggests that it is not said out of rancour or bitterness. The most common expression among people on the circuit (ie those applicants who meet each other at interviews for headships in different schools) is 'It's whether your face fits', which is another way of saying that your personality and management style must accord with those that the governors are looking for.

Having done your preliminary reading, and having made any discreet enquiries from whatever sources you have available, you are then in a position to write your letter of application. The box below includes Rachel's letter of application for the post of headteacher of The Best School, advertised in March 2020, the details of her present responsibilities; and a summary of her previous experience, both of which are referred to in her letter of application.

Rachel's application for the post of headteacher

Rachel's letter of application

I have pleasure in applying for the position of headteacher of The Best School. I attach my completed application form, a list of recent courses/publications, details of my present responsibilities and a brief note about my previous experience. In this letter I will set out some thoughts that I hope will be helpful in describing the type of headteacher I would like to be.

Personality and management style

I believe that the personal qualities I can offer include enthusiasm, ability to motivate and to lead, organizational skills, willingness to consider new ideas and the stamina to put them into practice. I care about people and I believe that this shows through in my dealings with staff and with students.

My preferred management style is to be proactive, tempering this with patience where needed, and to be consultative, while being decisive when necessary (delegation without dereliction). I do not believe in a 'hit-and-run' style of management, where one generates as much change as possible without seeing it through; change must be rooted in the school so that it does not become associated with one person.

The challenge of the next decade

The key issue for the next 10 years centres on the involvement of parents in the new 'all-age' schools. I believe that effective leadership is essential if teachers are to take on this new challenge successfully. It is vital that the perspectives of all participants – teachers, adults and young people – are considered so that all their needs can be met.

Doing this effectively will mean that all participants must be fully involved in decisions affecting them. I feel that a headteacher must be positive in responding to, and in initiating, changes in a way which give all staff both the competence and the confidence to implement them.

The volume and pace of change is such that it is only the continuation and development of the team approach to management that will, in my opinion, enable schools to provide the best possible education for all students. As a head of department and latterly as a deputy head I have worked with various groups of staff – departments, pastoral groups, committees, task forces – which has further reinforced my belief in this style of management.

The opportunity exists at The Best School to establish a clear management structure for the coming decade. I believe that a new headteacher will be in a very good position to develop such a structure.

The purpose of the school

It is my view that schools exist to develop the potential of all their students. In realizing this potential, they need to be aware of their shared sense of values, including concern for others and respect for their beliefs and cultures. Students learn by example; it is therefore important that they see teaching staff in a school showing these values in their daily interactions with each other. High expectations are essential if real achievements are to be created. I believe that education can make a real difference to the quality of a young person's life and that this lays a great responsibility on schools and on their leaders. Good management will lead to a good school, and it is ultimately the headteacher who must set the example by a positive management style.

Students should be encouraged to set themselves targets that stretch their abilities and to see education as a lifelong process. Such a view has a considerable bearing on the development of the 'all-age' school.

I realize that I have touched briefly on many complex issues. I would welcome the opportunity to discuss them at interview.

Yours sincerely,

Rachel Jones

Rachel's summary of her present post

Acacia School

Acacia School is an 11–18 mixed comprehensive school, with 980 students on roll; there are 190 students in the post-16 centre. The students come from a mixture of private and council-owned housing. We offer a complete range of post-16 courses, combining the academic and the vocational. There is a strong tradition of team management, which creates a purposeful and committed teaching staff.

The post

As a deputy headteacher I share overall management responsibility for the school, including deputizing for the headteacher as necessary and dealing with pastoral matters, both with staff and students. In addition, I have the following specific responsibilities.

Curriculum and staffing*. We have had a major review of the curriculum in anticipation of receiving our first intake of adults as the school becomes designated as 'all-age' in September 2021. I am responsible for recommending staffing needs to the governors' sub-committee, aided by a joint consultative group of governors and teaching staff.*

*All **staff development activities** are within my job description. I chair the meetings of the INSET committee, which agrees policy and makes recommendations for future budget needs to the governors' finance sub-committee. The appraisal committee was moved to my area of responsibility last year.*

Capitation*. Once the governors have decided the budget for capitation, I am completely responsible for its allocation. This is managed through a committee of staff, which makes recommendations to the headteacher. I am pleased that these have always been accepted, which indicates the professionalism with which the committee approaches the task.*

Governors' meetings*. I attend all governors' meetings and report on how I have managed the areas allocated to me. This has given me very real experience of this key area of headship.*

Rachel's summary of her previous experience

Great School, Stone LEA, 9/02–8/07

Taught English for five years, across age and ability range. In charge of Key Stage 3 assessment (temporary 'A' allowance). Temporary sixth-form tutor for one year. Secretary of cross-curricular task force on assessment.

Leafy School, Stone LEA, 9/07–8/12

Second in English department. Acting head of department to cover absence of another member of staff. Set up 'paired reading' scheme, involving the identification and training of sixth-form students to operate it. Member of task force set up to reorganize the library into a whole-school resources centre.

Fir School, Wood LEA, 9/12–8/16

Head of English department. Chair of heads of department and chair of appraisal committee. Member of finance committee. Secretary of Wood LEA's Heads of English group, which advises the LEA on policy issues. Member of the Curriculum Review Group, with representatives of governors and teaching staff; I reported to a full meeting of the governors on their recommendations.

Much of the material in this application is of necessity hypothetical; for example, we do not know what the key issues of 2020 will be, what exactly will be the role of LEAs, and so on. It is the general approach to writing the letter that is relevant, however, not the matters of detail contained in it.

First of all, Rachel decides to 'go for it' right at the beginning of her letter. Her personality comes across fairly clearly: she uses easily remembered phrases such as 'delegation without dereliction' which will help set her letter apart from the others. This may not be what the governors are looking for but she has presented herself clearly. At the very least she may save herself a visit to an interview at which it will become clear that they are looking for someone different; for example, the school may be in turmoil and the governors may feel, rightly or wrongly, that they need someone to calm it down, not to enthuse it.

Rachel also decides to keep her letter short, with her previous experience summarized succinctly on two other sheets. Notice that she gives more space to, and more detail of, recent experience. However, it can be to her advantage to reinforce the point that she has been teaching for a substantial period of time and has wide experience of dealing with whole-school issues and with governing bodies.

Ken's letter would look different in terms of his experience, but the same general points apply: present yourself and your philosophy, highlight your relevant experience, and where possible relate points to the school you are applying to.

The purpose of all that you have done so far is to get an interview. The next chapter deals with that final hurdle.

6 *The interview*

The interview is still the chief method of selection for teaching posts; it is unusual for schools to use some of the procedures adopted outside the profession such as psychometric tests or assessment centres, although that may well change in the future, at least for some senior appointments. The appointment of a headteacher has resulted in at least some governing bodies involving professional recruitment consultants in the process.

One other notable feature of the profession's approach to this stage of the appointment procedure is that it is usual for all candidates to be interviewed on the same day(s) and for a decision to be announced when the interviews are finished. In many other jobs, candidates do not meet each other and do not wait around for the results; they are notified by post or by telephone.

Invitation to interview

If you are called for interview, you may have between a week and a fortnight to make the arrangements. There are exceptions to this, especially when the so-called 'resignation dates' are approaching, when in fact you may get very short notice indeed. You should always reply to the invitation immediately, since many schools have a reserve list of candidates in the event of someone withdrawing before interview. You may well get a call at the last minute, which could indicate that you have been a reserve; once you get to interview, though, you should have the same chance as anyone else (provided that the post is genuinely an open one) and many candidates called in at the last minute like this have actually been appointed.

There are some general practices about being called for interview, which are summarized below. (Please note that there are always exceptions, particularly now that governors, with their experience of alternative methods of appointment, are responsible for appointments.)

General practices for interviews

▌ Schools will normally call between four (for posts with one or two responsibility points) and 10 (for deputy headships and headships) candidates. Travel expenses will be paid. However, these will often be at minimal rates (eg second-class rail fare) and will often not be paid if a candidate refuses an offer of appointment.

▌ Accommodation expenses are usually paid at even more minimal rates and you may be given an upper limit; you will normally have to make your own arrangements.

▌ If you teach in a shortage subject, do not be surprised to be telephoned by the headteacher – and remember that first impressions count!

▌ A tour of the school – and a chance to meet at least some staff – is usual. Sometimes this can be done before the day of interview. Paid leave of absence to attend for interview is normal practice. You may be sent a map to help you find the school, but don't be surprised if you are not.

Pre-interview preparation

If you are called for interview it is important to organize yourself properly if you are to do yourself justice. Check all the details in the letter, ensuring, for example, that the day and date of interview match up; it is not unheard of for schools to send out an invitation with the wrong details. If you find a discrepancy, telephone to find out the correct details; check before you do so, since you may acquire a reputation for inefficiency before you even get there if the mistake is yours and not theirs.

It is *de rigueur* for men to wear a suit to interview; choose a style that you feel comfortable in, but remember that teaching is a conservative profession. Before Parliament was televised a lot of attention was paid to advising MPs on what colour of suit to wear; I would not presume to judge on such an issue except to say that you should try to ensure that your appearance reflects your personality.

Women have greater choice in what they should wear, which of course presents a greater dilemma. As the profession becomes more managerial in its culture, it would appear that suits are becoming more popular among women attending for interview. This is not to say that women should wear suits, merely to observe that there seems to be a trend towards it.

For both sexes, it is probably wise to pay some attention to general grooming; again, this is a matter of personal taste, but take a critical look in the mirror before deciding not to bother visiting the hairdresser.

White shirts or blouses are usually a safe enough bet but the colour of a tie can be important. It is useful to know the colours associated with the main political parties; some would say that to wear a red tie to an interview in an area dominated by Conservative councillors (or a blue tie in a Labour-dominated area) would be unwise. There is no evidence for this – and such a hypothesis is unlikely to be easy to research – but if you feel there may be some truth in it, it is wise to play safe and avoid the particular colour concerned.

The general point is that your appearance will have an effect, possibly subconscious and therefore more powerful, on interviewers. The simple rule is to ensure that you present the image you intend to. Research indicates that only 7 per cent of impact at an interview can be attributed to the content of what is said by the interviewee: 38 per cent is attributable to voice (accent, use of grammar, overall confidence) and no less than 55 per cent is attributable to visual impact. You have been warned! (A useful thing might be to check the advice you would give to a 16-year old school leaver about interview technique – and then apply it to your own situation!)

Reading

It is important that you prepare yourself mentally by reading both the job details (including any information about the school) and your application. You need to read the details several times so that you can answer general questions in an intelligent way. Many heads will not take kindly to you displaying your igno- rance about something mentioned in the job details, even if this is only to say how long the school has been open.

The night before an interview is not the time to try to catch up with all the educational reading you have been meaning to do for the past two months. Regular reading is much more likely to be of use in that you will be up to date with current thinking in your subject area (where applicable) and in education in general. It is more useful to find your own ways of relaxing than to stay up late, which will make you feel tired the next morning.

Getting there

You need to make a realistic assessment of how long it will take to get to the school on the day of the interview – and then add some time to allow for delays. Unless it is local, there is a good chance that it will be difficult to get there by public transport, and a two-hour drive on the morning of an interview is not the best preparation. On the other hand, you may prefer to be at home the night before rather than to stay in a cheap hotel (based on the level of expenses paid in most areas).

If you are likely to have to stay overnight, then you should plan the practical details – such as clothing and personal effects to be taken – before you are called for interview. It is better to make a list of what you will need for an interview when you start applying for jobs; once you have begun the process of applying, there is a good chance you will need this list, and you will have enough to think about without having to worry about such basic details.

Arrival

Earlier in the book we noted that any telephone call to the school could affect your chances of being appointed. This point needs to be taken further: you are on interview from the moment you arrive at the school. There is no such thing as a breathing space between arriving and being interviewed.

The formal interview will come at the end of the day (or days) but do not underestimate the influence of anyone you speak to in the school, be it an adult or a child. The way you introduce yourself at the main office, even the way you drive into the school, may affect your chances of getting the post. This is not fanciful, it is reality. If you nearly knock down a pupil on your way in, word will spread; if you mumble at the office, word will spread; if you are rude to anyone, you may have finished your chances altogether. You need to strike a balance between diffidence and arrogance. There is a saying that can be helpful for these initial stages: 'If in doubt, say nowt.'

The best advice I was given about interviews is 'Be relaxed'. This is very difficult to achieve but can be made easier by one's mental attitude. If you desperately want the post, it will be harder to be relaxed; on the other hand, if you are too relaxed about things you may give the impression that you don't want the post at all. This is why your overall attitude to your application needs to be right in the first place. If the interview is the result of three or more years of planning, you will know that even if you do not get this post, another suitable one may appear quite soon afterwards.

Tour of the school

Although there are many variations on the theme, there will be very few interviews that do not include some sort of tour of the school. Most schools will try to make this as realistic as possible. There may be an introductory talk from the head and/or other members of staff, followed probably by a formal tour and possibly an informal tour as well, sometimes with pupils assigned to show you round. This is your chance to ask intelligent questions, to look as carefully as you can at relationships between staff and pupils; in short to decide if you want to teach there. It is not unheard of, incidentally, for pupils to be sounded out about the candidate(s) they have shown round.

If you go into a classroom you should try to look interested in what the children are doing. While one candidate is trying to convince everybody that he or she knows everything there is to know about education, this is your chance to find out what makes the place tick. Asking children questions can have two benefits: first, you will get information and second, it may be reported back to the head that you actually show an interest in them!

Some schools ask candidates to teach – and some involve students in part of the pre-interviewing process. If this happens, it is important to be yourself, keep calm and use the opportunity to find out a bit more about how the school operates. Remember, also, that students smell fear from a distance!

If you are not shown round the school – or your trip misses out certain areas – be suspicious but do not necessarily jump to conclusions. It could be that efforts are being made to cut down the walking or to get to the interviews quickly, but it could also be that something is being hidden. Be alert to signs of the latter and do not be afraid to ask questions. Listen also to the answers given to the questions of other candidates, both for their content and for clues as to the general ethos of the school.

It is usual for lunch to be provided – and candidates rarely have to pay for it these days. However, sometimes you will be left to your own devices. In the absence of specific details in advance it does no harm to have some emergency provision so that you are not weak from hunger by the time of your interview! The vast majority of schools are staffed by thoughtful people, who will offer you lunch and coffee, show you where the toilets are, and so on. However, sometimes details like these are overlooked and it does no harm to be prepared.

Beware of drinking too much tea or coffee. If you are offered alcohol with lunch I would advise that you decline it, since most people find that it does not enhance their performance at interview. Avoid smoking during the day if you can.

The school ethos

You need to make up your mind fairly quickly about whether you like the school or not. Below are some questions you can ask yourself. The answers to some will have been in the job details (in which case you are looking for confirmation that what was said on paper applies in practice), while the answers to many of the others can be gleaned without actually having to ask them.

Checklist to assess school compatibility

- Do the children seem purposeful in most classes?
- How do they behave outside lessons?
- Do I feel comfortable with the staff and children? Can I relate to the school ethos? Will my teaching methods fit in?
- Is there a definite staff development policy?
- Is the school on the way up or the way down? Are pupil numbers steady?
- Are there are budget problems which might lead to staffing reductions?
- Are staff friendly with each other?
- Does the reality of the school match up with the job details? For example, is the atmosphere really one of cooperation?
- What consultative procedures exist? Will they allow me to participate in decision-making?

This list is not exhaustive and there will be many other questions that you will wish to add. It is important to remember that the selection process should be a two-way one. You should be prepared to withdraw from consideration if you do not feel happy about the school. Most schools will pay your expenses if you do withdraw – if you do so before they actually offer you the post – but even where they do not, you must be prepared to suffer the loss of expenses if you are not happy. Trying to 'fail' the interview as an alternative has two main drawbacks: first, you may not manage to do this and secondly, you may jeopardize your chances of being interviewed for a subsequent post in the same area. Only once when I withdrew from an interview – because information provided in advance did not accord with other evidence on the day – did the LEA refuse to pay my expenses and I have never regretted my action for one minute. It is foolish to expect to find the absolutely perfect school, but a high degree of compatibility is essential for continued sanity.

Interview patterns

I have mentioned that the number of candidates interviewed is likely to be greater for more senior posts. It may be helpful to look at the likely patterns for different levels, with the caveat that these are only generalizations and do not always apply, especially in these days of LMS (Local Management of Schools).

First posts

A school looking to fill a post for a classroom teacher may well choose to interview between three and six candidates. It is also likely that there will be a tour of the school in the morning, with the interviews in the afternoon. If an appointment is to be made, the result will almost certainly be announced shortly after the interviews are completed. This means, of course, that if you are interviewed at 1 pm you may then have to wait until 4 pm or much later for the result. One interview of between 20 and 30 minutes is the norm. The interviewing panel will vary but one consisting of the head, the head of department, an LEA adviser and a member of the governing body is not unusual.

Middle management posts

For a post at head of department level the process is likely to be fairly similar to that used for first posts. However, for posts that carry senior management responsibilities (with, say, three or more responsibility points) the procedures adopted for deputy head appointments may be applied.

The place of the head of department on the interviewing panel may be filled by the outgoing head of department or by a deputy head. There may be a larger panel and in some cases there may be preliminary interviews. The box below sets out the order of the day that applies in at least some schools, where the decision-making process involves more than the small panel referred to above. Once again, it does need to be emphasized that there is no one way of appointing, but fashions are inclined to spread.

All your discussions, including the meeting with staff at break time and lunch with the interviewing panel, should be treated as part of your interview. There is a growing awareness in schools that good interpersonal relationships, especially those between staff, are important to a successful school. The informal settings can also be used to complement the answers given in the formal interview in the afternoon.

Once your interview is over you will normally be free to stay or leave, provided that you return for the announcement of the result. What you do is a matter of personal choice, but if you do leave make sure that you get back in plenty of time.

In the example given below, the fact that the deputy head (curriculum) is involved in the morning session may indicate that the other deputy head will be taking part in the formal interviews in the afternoon (or it may just mean that she or he is absent).

Timetable for appointment of head of Geography

9.15. Arrival of (four) candidates. Coffee and introductory welcome by head.

9.30. Two groups (A, B) to rotate round the following activities:
tour of school (20 minutes);
meeting with some heads of department (20 minutes);
Coffee in Staff room (10.10–10.30);
meeting with some pastoral heads (20 minutes);

> meeting with deputy head (curriculum) (20 minutes);
> meeting with present head of department (20 minutes).
>
> 11.30. Question and answer session with head.
>
> 11.50. Lunch with interviewing panel.
>
> 1.00. Panel meets to discuss questions for interviews.
>
> 1.15. Interviews (approximately 30 minutes each).
>
> 3.45. Announcement of result.

Deputy head posts

The norm for deputy head appointments is a two-day process. It is also usual to call initially six to eight candidates (the so-called 'long list'), with preliminary interviews on the first day intended to produce a short-list of three or four for the formal interviews on the second day. The process in many ways mirrors that used for the appointment of headteachers, at least in some parts of the country. A typical timetable for a deputy head appointment is set out below, with the usual proviso that it may be typical only in being untypical.

> ### Timetable for appointment of deputy head
>
> *Day one*
>
> 10.00. Arrival (eight candidates) and coffee. Welcome by head.
>
> 10.30. Tour of school in two groups.
>
> 11.30. Question and answer session with head.
>
> 12.00. Lunch.
>
> 1.00. Preliminary interviews with three panels.
>
> 4.30. Announcement of names of candidates chosen for formal interviews on day two.
>
> *Day two*
>
> 9.30. Interviews (approximately 30 minutes each).
>
> 12.00. Announcement of result.

Much of the detail has been omitted here; for example, one would expect detailed timings and membership of groups for tours of school. The intention of this timetable is to give an idea of the experience one may face in being interviewed for this level of post.

The informal interviews on day one are likely to be carried out by small panels of two or three people, including possibly the present deputy heads, some governors (including teacher-governors) and advisers. The final panel may consist of only four people but equally it may consist of more than that, especially if the governors are keen to be fully involved in the process. The warning that has already been given – that you are on interview all the time – still applies.

Headship posts

If LMS altered the way appointments are made to other posts in schools, it totally changed what one can expect when applying for a headship. Previously, LEAs had their own way of making such appointments (which varied considerably even then), but at least one could predict what would happen in particular parts of the country. It was not unusual for a short-listed but unsuccessful candidate for one headship in a particular LEA to be appointed to the next vacancy in that LEA. This gave some semblance of predictability, both for LEAs and applicants. Equally, failure to impress a particular LEA the first time might well have precluded the candidate from obtaining another interview in that area.

Now that governors are responsible for making such appointments – taking into consideration the views of the LEA, but not bound by them – any predictability has gone completely. Anecdotal evidence suggests that this change, added to the drastic speed of innovation in schools, has resulted in more 'safe' appointments (ie of candidates who are older and/or known to the LEA) than previously. However, such evidence is anecdotal and should not stop you from applying for posts that match with your specific qualifications and experience.

There is no typical pattern of appointment at this level. In some areas the governors rely very much on the LEA (particularly the officers) to set out the timetable and format for the appointment, while in others each school goes its own way. Interviews, particularly the preliminary ones, are sometimes held in the school and sometimes in the Town Hall or Professional Centre. In most cases, expect to be interviewed by up to 20 people. Some methods of appointment to headships that have been used recently are set out below. They illustrate the point made above that the only pattern is a lack of one.

Some methods used for headship appointments

▌ *Post A.* Three-day process. Six candidates given a personal, hour-long tour of the school by the chair of governors on day one. Each candidate to make a 20-minute presentation to the governors (on pre-notified topic) on day two. Three candidates called for one-hour interview on day three. (Each of the three days was separated by a week.)

▌ *Post B.* Twenty candidates called for preliminary interview. Each one invited to arrange with the present incumbent to see round school on the afternoon prior to their interviews (which were held with LEA officers on several different dates). Four candidates (including two who had been interviewed for a previous post in the LEA but not for the present one) were called for formal interview with the governors.

▌ *Post C.* Six candidates called for interview. Visit to school on an afternoon, followed by informal meeting with the governors over tea and biscuits. Formal interview with the full governing body, plus LEA officers and including teacher-governors, on the next day. All six candidates called for formal interview.

▌ *Post D.* Personal visit to school, to be shown round by present incumbent (including in one case a visit on a Saturday, accompanied by spouse). Informal interviews on day one proper, followed by tea and biscuits with some of the interviewing panel. Formal interview for all short-listed candidates on day two.

> ▌ *Post E.* Long-list of twelve candidates called for day one. Shorter list of six called for day two. Final short-list of three called for day three.
>
> ▌ *Post F.* Eight candidates called on day one. Four visited school in morning while others were being interviewed, with the procedure being reversed for the other four. (Yes – some were interviewed before they had visited the school!) Short-list of four notified by post for second day, formal, interviews.

It should be emphasized that these are all based on real cases. Although some of them might raise a few eyebrows, it is unlikely that any one stands out from the rest as being more successful in making the right appointment. What is seen as the norm – in any part of the country – is not necessarily the most effective way to make what is the most important appointment for any school.

Assessment centres

There is a developing interest in the use of assessment centres and/or consultancy services for headship appointments in this country. However, it is probably only a matter of time before at least some methods used by assessment centres – for example, psychometric tests – are used by schools.

Succession management

The idea of succession planning – or succession management as it is now becoming styled in the business world – is beginning to gain some favour in education. Such an idea works on the basis of identifying suitable candidates for headship at early stages of their careers and trying to organize their experience and training to equip them for headship in the future.

Interviews

At its simplest, an interview involves the selection panel asking questions of the candidates and listening to their answers. It is universally used in teaching as the basis of making appointments. Therefore, one's interview technique is critical if one is to be appointed. I know of one instance where a candidate who did not perform well at interview was offered a 'debriefing' on her interview performance. The job was re-advertised and she got the job next time round. There are instances where the 'gut feeling' of a panel will overrule their perception of a poor performance at interview but this is not common. Some general advice on interview technique will be given, but before that it may be useful to look at different types of interview and some other refinements which are used from time to time.

'In tray' exercises

In some cases, candidates are given simulations of situations they may have to deal with if appointed. Examples would include a member of staff who has not marked exercise books (how would a head of department deal with this?), an irate parent complaining about a teacher (how would a deputy head deal with this?), or differences of opinion between the staff and governors (how would a head deal with this?). Sometimes one may be presented with several items, all of which are urgent, and asked to prioritize action to be taken.

Written responses to these exercises may be sought, or they may be discussed at interview, or both. The idea behind their use is to give some insight into how the candidates would react to their new responsibilities. The safest advice is to be calm, be consistent with what you have said in your application and be legible in any written tasks you undertake.

Group discussions

Some schools have experimented with group discussions, where the candidates are given an issue – for example, assessment under the National Curriculum – and observed while they discuss it. The problem with this, for both the interviewers and the candidates, is that few teachers are properly equipped to make any meaningful comments about such interactions. For the candidate, a balance needs to be struck between being too dominant and not saying anything. Whether this practice will increase or not is difficult to say.

Informal interviews

The use of the word 'informal' usually indicates that the interviewers are trying to put candidates at their ease and that there is a two-way process of selection at work. Sensible panels recognize that some candidates may not find their school's ethos compatible with their own and are keen that they are given the opportunity to say so.

Important advice for this kind of interview centres around two issues. First of all, you must be yourself: it is silly to try to guess what the interviewers are looking for, except where small details are concerned. Secondly, do not be fooled into thinking that the informality will minimize the effect of anything you say: in fact, a skilful interviewer will draw out your views in an informal interview far more easily than in a formal interview.

Formal interviews

Very few appointments to teaching posts are made nowadays without a formal interview. The composition of the panels may vary but the process is still one of asking questions and eliciting responses. Some general tips are given below, but remember that an interview is a very complicated piece of social interaction. For example, the candidate does not know who on the panel carries most weight, whether the support of the LEA officer will be a bonus or a liability, or how nervous some members of the panel will be (especially members of the governing body – some parent-governors will find interviewing prospective heads a harrowing experience).

Interview tips

▌ The first few minutes are crucial – try to feel relaxed.

▌ You should look at the person asking the question and listen carefully before giving your answer. If you are unsure about the question, either clarify it before answering or answer the question you think you are being asked and then check that this is what was intended.

▌ Do not give monosyllabic answers if you can avoid it.

▌ Try to relate your answer to your experience by giving examples of what you have done.

▌ False modesty impresses nobody. If you do not tell the panel what you have done, no one else will. Be wary of arrogance, however.

▌ Do not patronize the questioner.

▌ Be ready with your answer to the usual last question, 'Are you still a serious candidate for the post?' (Your answer should not be sycophantic, but equally try to project at least a little enthusiasm into your affirmation. Do not, however, go on to give a whole list of reasons why you are still interested.)

▌ Remember that, in teaching at any rate, more people talk their way out of jobs than into them. Desperation will not succeed.

▌ Psychologists suggest that most interviewers form an impression of a candidate within the first few minutes and that afterwards they are subconsciously looking for reasons to confirm their opinion. If this is the case, the first minutes are the crucial ones.

▌ Keep calm. If the interview is a long one, taking a (small) drink of water, if provided, can help slow you down and give you time to think. If you do take a drink, don't rush or you risk spilling it!

Whatever level of post you are applying for in teaching you are going to have to demonstrate competent communication skills, whether with students or staff. In some schools, applicants for head of department posts may be asked to demonstrate their teaching ability – usually with a fairly 'tame' class. Therefore the main way of testing this important skill is through the interview.

Questions

There are different types of questions that are asked at interviews. Below are some of them.

Types of interview question

▌ Putting candidates at their ease.

▌ Checking up and/or confirming information from the written application.

▌ Testing candidates' knowledge of subject.

▌ Testing candidates' knowledge of current educational topics.

▌ Ascertaining management skills (eg ability to work in a team; to lead a department).

▌ Establishing the personality of the applicant.

▌ Checking if the applicant is still interested in the post.

The first questioner may ask the candidate to outline briefly his or her career to date. This will, of course, already be written down but many panels feel that this question helps candidates to relax. Be succinct, spend most time on your recent experience, and do not try to anticipate questions further on in the interview.

Your knowledge of your subject may be tested by very specific questions (particularly if there is an adviser present); for example, a candidate for an English post might be asked to state their current reading or favourite writer. Make sure that any information you give is accurate.

Knowledge of current educational issues (for example, National Curriculum and assessment) may be assumed by some panels but not by others. Keeping up with educational theory about your subject – and thinking intelligently about how such theory can be put into practice – is the best way of ensuring that these questions do not cause you any problems. Relate your answers to your current practice or previous experience.

It is in the area of checking the management skills and/or personality of the candidates that the more esoteric questions are asked. As fast as candidates learn these questions – and prepare their 'model' answers – interviewers think of others. The whole point of this type of question is to try to get past the 'interview veneer' and find the real person underneath. I do not propose to give such 'model' answers here, since they would contradict the philosophy of this book that you should clarify your own thinking and then communicate it to others. However, here are some (real) questions which I have either been asked or been told of. If nothing else, they may show the variety on offer!

Some questions asked at interviews

▌ Are you motivated by money?

▌ If your doctor told you that you had 24 hours to live, what would you do?

▌ How do you spend your spare time?

▌ How do you deal with stress?

▌ Do you think your (lack of) height will affect your ability to maintain discipline in the classroom?

▌ How often do you pray? (In an interview for an Aided School.)

▌ Who has been the greatest influence on your life?

▌ Can you tell me a book I should read?

No amount of preparation can help you with this type of question. When one comes your way, you need to pause for thought and then give an honest answer.

One other point worth making about interviews is that humour can be used to great advantage in certain situations. However, you need to be careful. Good advice is to use any informal setting – for example, a meeting with the panel over tea or lunch – to gauge what will be seen as appropriate and what will not.

It is usual for panels to ask candidates if they have any questions. If there are points about which you are not clear, now is the time to ask about them. Do not feel that you have to ask a question – it is perfectly acceptable to say, 'Thank you, but I have had all my questions answered during the day.' It is also normal to be asked if you are still a firm candidate for the post. A simple 'Yes, very much so' is fine; alternatively you may wish to withdraw, in which case it is important to keep things simple. (You are best withdrawing before the final interview!)

Appointment

The normal way of announcing the result of the interview is for one of the panel – often the adviser, since no one really enjoys this part of the process – to check that all the candidates are together and then to say something like, 'The panel would like to speak to Mr or Ms X.' This may be prefaced with remarks explaining the difficulty of making a decision (which may well be true, in spite of the cynicism with which such announcements are usually treated).

Mr or Ms X will be whisked off to meet the panel and everyone else will wait, hopefully for only a few minutes, until they are told that the post has been offered, has been accepted and that forms are available for claiming expenses. Do not go before this happens: Mr or Ms X may not accept the post (unlikely at this stage but still possible). It is easier to sort out how to get your expenses if you ask at this point, and you need to clarify if a 'debriefing' is on offer.

Debriefing

It has become a fairly common practice to offer unsuccessful candidates for posts at all levels a 'debriefing'. This is often given by LEA officers, mainly because very few people actually want to do it. The purpose is to suggest to unsuccessful candidates the reasons why they did not get the post and to make suggestions about how they can go about improving their chances of getting the next post they apply for.

There are different opinions on the value of such an exercise. One view is that the whole method of selecting candidates for teaching posts is corrupt and that debriefing only gives it a false legitimacy. However, it has to be said that many people find a debriefing helpful, if only to confirm their suitability for the type of post they are seeking. In my own experience, I have learnt a great deal from two such exercises and would say that if it is offered it is worth taking. Even if it is not offered, it may be worth asking for advice, particularly from LEA officers or sympathetic heads. Make clear that you are genuinely seeking advice, not trying to argue that the appointment process was in some way flawed!

After the interview

If you are successful, ensure that you get a written job offer before resigning from your present post. If you are unsuccessful, do remember that it is not the end of the world, and can be a very useful learning experience. Even though it sometimes sounds improbable, old hands will tell you that, if you want a particular level of post above everything else, perseverance will pay off eventually. The last bit is important: if you want more than one thing at a time (for example, a headship and an idyllic cottage in the Lake District), you may have to settle for just one of them! The most important thing to remember is that you should be in control of your life.

7 Development strategies

Much of this book has been written on the assumption that the reader will be looking for promotion. However, not every teacher wants promotion, which often means less time in the classroom. If you are not seeking promotion, or if you have not decided if you want promotion, this final chapter looks at how to keep yourself fresh and takes a detached look at the advantages and drawbacks of typical promotion moves in the profession.

Personal development

The most important thing to bear in mind is that, whether you intend to seek promotion or not, it is essential – for the sake of both you and the young people under your influence – to keep fresh. Earlier in the book it was pointed out that promotion almost always involves attendance at courses and further study. It is perhaps unfortunate that in the past this was very often the most useful element of participating in such activities!

The profession needs to ensure that all teachers, particularly those who do not want promotion, are enthusiastic, well trained and highly motivated. The only satisfactory way of ensuring this is to create an environment in which teachers want to develop their skills and feel actively involved in the process. The culture of the individual school will have a lot to do with this, which is a particularly strong reason for making sure that you teach in a school which allows you to feel confident in your abilities; such self-confidence is a prerequisite for recognizing that improvement is always possible.

The most important way of ensuring that you continue to approach teaching with a fresh mind is not to centre your whole life on it. Unless you lift your head from the hurly-burly of the classroom and school, it is difficult to maintain the vision of what is possible. This is another way of saying that the most important prerequisite of professional development is personal development. Teachers need to be people in their own right and not just automatons who appear to spend all their lives in school. One hopes there will be greater encouragement for teachers to take sabbaticals.

Opportunities for short-term sabbaticals are increasingly becoming available, but the funding for sabbaticals for all is a long time coming. Many teachers have gone straight into the profession from higher education and have become locked into the inflexibility of the present system. A sabbatical for every teacher for, say, a term every 10 years could be one strategy for ensuring that all teachers are lively and enthusiastic.

Professional development

Personal development is a prerequisite for professional development, but it is not enough in itself. The skills and knowledge required for teaching effectively are always changing in response both to research into what makes for effective learning and to the development of new technologies to assist with the learning process. We can look briefly at some of the methods for ensuring that you do indeed keep up to date.

It should be said at this point that keeping up to date is important for all staff. It is as crucial for heads, for example, to engage in self-review as it is for classroom teachers. There are several general ways in which all members of the profession can try to ensure that they continue to improve their effectiveness.

By far the easiest way of keeping up to date is to read regularly about education. The general trends are easily followed in the *Times Educational Supplement,* and most of the quality national daily and weekly newspapers carry educational articles. The

Internet has several Web sites that make it easy to keep up with the news on a daily basis.

For information about a particular subject area, membership of a subject association (eg the Association for Science Education) is valuable; such associations customarily have publications that are beneficial for the individual member and they often organize conferences and courses. The cost of membership of a subject association can usually be set against tax. There are often useful programmes on television, although unfortunately these are often populist (giving such a broad coverage for the general viewer that they are not helpful for the specialist) or politicized.

The teacher professional associations/unions have also been involved in the professional development of their members. In many parts of the country there are local associations for specific groups of staff, for example heads of science, deputy heads, and so on. Good LEAs are often in a position to put on courses and updating sessions for staff in their area. They can often be a very good way of sharing ideas and solving problems.

Courses

In the past there were teachers who never attended courses. It is harder to do this now, although it is a sad reflection on the quality of many courses that there are still teachers who would avoid them if they could. A good course can have two major benefits: first, you can update professional skills, and secondly, you can meet other teachers and learn from them through informal discussion. We will look at performance management later but in theory at least, individual teachers identify their training needs in discussion with their team leader. There are many courses available – from a wide range of providers – which go some way to meet the various needs of teachers.

Many courses last for between one day and one week, with some move towards residential elements. Such courses offer opportunities for subject updating or the development of specific skills, such as teambuilding. They should be a regular feature of the average teacher's development, with most teachers going on such a course annually.

One very beneficial way of giving a fresh perspective on teaching is to undertake a 'teacher placement'. The value of such placements has somewhat belatedly been recognized by the provision of some government finance to assist this. Most teachers who have undertaken (properly prepared) placements attest to their value.

The government is currently encouraging teachers to look for opportunities to undertake placements and/or training abroad. These opportunities can be very worthwhile, both for the individual teacher and for his/her school.

Accreditation

There is a strong case for teachers undertaking study leading to some form of accreditation at several points during their career. It used to be that the only way of getting further qualifications was to study full time for an advanced diploma or a higher degree such as MEd or PhD. Apart from the fact that many teachers have no real desire to take a year off school, higher degrees were often irrelevant not only to teachers' needs but also to those of the school.

It is now possible to take units or modules, with a specific qualification being awarded after the accumulation of a certain number. This is helping to encourage teachers to do relatively short courses of study (eg six to 10 hours a week over a term), which are directly relevant to their own perceived training needs and/or those of their schools. It is important for the quality of teaching that such courses are not seen exclusively as stepping stones to promotion. It is also important that schools encourage such professional development by funding courses. Local Management of Schools (LMS) allows schools much more freedom to do this.

Teachers – particularly those who are members of the leadership team – are being encouraged to undertake the NPQH (National Professional Qualification for Headship). It is the intention of the government that in the future all prospective headteachers will have to possess the NPQH before they can be considered.

Performance management

The introduction of the upper pay spine for teachers has been accompanied by the requirement that all teachers must take part in a regular performance management system. This has been accompanied by training for headteachers and team leaders. Each governing body must use the services of an external adviser to discuss the progress of the headteacher each year. This procedure is being used to ensure that schools keep their performance management systems going.

From the point of view of teachers, it is vital that performance management is seen as an opportunity to analyse their progress, to identify training needs and to have them met. Appraisal is potentially a vital resource. Self-awareness is needed if you are to improve your skills as a teacher. A good performance management system will allow this self-awareness to be developed. In some cases it will lead to thoughts of promotion and in others it will reinforce a commitment to classroom teaching: in all cases it will hopefully lead to a continuous self-analysis and self-improvement by individuals and by schools.

What does promotion entail?

Before thinking about promotion it is important to have some idea of what it entails. Obviously it is possible to look at existing post-holders and see what they do. However, this does not necessarily give the whole picture. Apart from the fact that your experience of role models may then be limited to one school, the way in which one head of department, for example, does the job does not necessarily dictate the way you would approach the same job, either in your present school or in a different one. The intention here is to suggest some of the responsibilities which typical post-holders take on when they accept a promotion, so that you have a starting-point for your own thinking.

Personality

Your personality is important and certain posts do require particular skills, but it is essential that you do not assume that every person must have a superhuman range of innate talent to be able to take on promotion. Very many teachers are quite capable of taking on these responsibilities if they are trained to do so.

If you feel it might be useful, it could be worth taking a psychometric test. In itself this is unlikely to be able to tell you whether you will do well in a particular post but it can be helpful in deciding whether you have the particular range of qualities needed for certain posts. However, it is worth bearing in mind that the increasing emphasis in schools on team approaches to work can mean that one person does not have to possess all the qualities needed for, say, headship, provided that she or he can ensure that someone else in the team takes on the things which the head does not do very well.

Middle management

There is a wide range of posts that fall under the general heading of 'middle management', ranging from head of department in a secondary school to teacher responsible for science, literacy or ICT in a primary school. However, they share certain key characteristics. If you are thinking about applying for such a post, you need to think about the following kinds of responsibility and whether you are prepared to take them on.

▌ Administration. This should not be overestimated and many schools now see the value of employing adequate support staff; however, there are bound to be forms to fill in for all sorts of things.

- Chairing meetings. This is a skill that can be learnt; some middle managers do this well, while others do not. Basics include ensuring that there is an agenda, that all topics are covered and that individuals all get the opportunity to contribute.
- Managing people. This is the key to all the other responsibilities. Good interpersonal skills are essential, but they can be learnt.
- Taking responsibility for delegated areas. Sometimes this will entail apologizing for things done (or, more likely, omitted) by others than yourself. Effective delegation is the answer.
- Management of finance allocated to your department or subject area.
- Representing a collective view to senior management, school advisers, parents, governors, etc.
- Carrying out within your area of responsibility decisions taken elsewhere, even when you were not in agreement with the decision(s) in the first place.
- Production of schemes of work. Dealing with queries about examination or test results.
- Acting as first line when there are difficulties with pupils in classrooms in your subject area.

One thing which management responsibility does not – or at least should not – entail is ordering people about. You do carry greater power but this is usually only exercised effectively in a democratic, not autocratic, manner.

Senior management and the leadership team

The term 'senior management', or 'leadership team', was traditionally used specifically in relation to secondary as opposed to primary schools; however, many primary schools do have such groupings. In the secondary school, it is likely to include not only deputy heads (who we will look at shortly) and assistant heads but also those holding four promotion points. In addition to the responsibilities listed under the previous section, members of senior management or leadership teams are likely to have to carry out one or more of the following:

▌ Oversight of a whole area – curricular, pastoral or physical – of the school.
▌ Duty systems, such as supervision of the playground at break-times.
▌ Attendance at meetings with governors or parents. Membership of groups charged with looking at whole-school policies, such as assessment.
▌ Supervision of the work of some middle managers.

The nature and scope of responsibility are greater at this level and you are likely to become involved in more meetings. You have greater influence at an early stage when ideas are being mooted but you are more likely to be called upon to convey decisions with which you may not fully agree. You will need to be the type of person who enjoys this kind of participation – or at least does not mind it too much – if you are to find such a post personally and professionally rewarding.

Deputy headship and assistant headship

Deputy heads – and in many cases, assistant heads – carry the responsibilities already identified for the other promoted posts but are also likely to:

▌ Teach less. Will you miss your previous level of contact with the pupils?
▌ Take the lead in translating the decisions of others (head and/or staff committee) into effective actions – this is sometimes called 'carrying the can'.

■ Spend more time dealing with parents, the community and governors.

There are two particular points to be made about deputy headship (both primary and secondary) that may be seen to be two sides of the same coin. First, your conditions of service are different from those of other teachers, particularly with regard to 1,265 hours. They set you out as carrying the same level of responsibility as the headteacher, particularly if the head is out of school. The buck may well stop with you, whether over the decision about what to do with fog falling rapidly on the school or about intruders on the premises. Secondly, you are not the head and therefore the only final decisions which you make are those that are delegated to you, usually in the short term. This raises two important questions: Do you want to carry the ultimate responsibility in the absence of the head? Would you find it frustrating being so near the final decision without actually making it?

You also have to decide whether you would wish to remain as a deputy head if you do not choose to apply for headship (or apply without success). The step to deputy headship is not one to be taken lightly; no one else can decide whether this is a step you wish to take, which is why so much emphasis has been placed on self-awareness in this book. (To gain further insight into exactly what being a deputy head in a secondary school can involve, you may wish to read my _Handbook for Deputy Heads_, 2nd edition, 1997, published by Kogan Page.)

Assistant heads in many cases share the same kind of responsibilities that deputy heads carry, without being required to stand in for the headteacher. Therefore, most of the points made about deputy headship also apply to assistant headship.

Headship

In some ways being a head is little different from being a deputy head in a school where you are fully involved in decision-making. Speaking personally, I have not found myself undertaking roles or tasks as a head that I had not already undertaken as a deputy head.

Having said this, it may appear paradoxical to say that being a headteacher is completely different from any other post in the school. The reasons for saying this are:

- The final decision lies with the head, as does the responsibility for setting the school 'vision'.
- The head has far more control over his or her working life than anyone else in the school, can decide what is to be delegated and what is not, which areas of responsibility to keep and how far to become involved in particular matters.
- Even at primary level, the teaching role is secondary to the management of staff. Pupil progress – the *raison d'être* of the school – will be achieved through other staff, rather than by personal interaction with the pupils.

Personality

Even the most cursory observation of existing heads suggests that there is no one personality type that suits the job. However, research indicates that effective heads share particular qualities. These include:

- strong personal values;
- commitment to achieving goals that they identify as important for their schools;
- the ability to focus staff and pupil efforts on achieving agreed goals;
- willingness to try new organizational methods;
- constant focus on a better future – setting the tone of continuous improvement.

It can be seen that these requirements still allow for vast differences in temperament and personality among headteachers.

If you decide that you are prepared to take on the responsibilities that go with the post, you need to give very careful thought to the exact nature of key relationships in the schools to which you are applying. These key relationships are with the governors (and particularly the chair of governors), staff (teaching and non-teaching alike), and parents and the community in general. If you are not comfortable with these relationships your life – and probably theirs as well – will be very difficult. It is therefore vital that in deciding to apply for a post, in going through with the interview process and in accepting the post if offered, you present very clearly your own views and your own management style: there is no point in pretending to be somebody other than yourself at this stage of your career.

Updating

The general rule about updating yourself personally and professionally applies as much to headship as to any other post. In addition, you have to make a decision at some point as to whether you intend to stay in your present post or move to another one, whether as a head elsewhere or to a different type of post. If you decide not to do this, then it is advisable to carry out a major personal review of your progress at least every few years.

Performance management can help you set your professional targets regularly in addition to carrying out your own personal review. If you write these down, it will be easier to see if you are achieving them.

National College for School Leadership

The National College for School Leadership (NCSL) was established to take responsibility for the leadership of potential, newly appointed and existing headteachers. The college is responsible for ensuring that there is a coherent programme, not for delivering all the activities itself. There are three main areas of development.

1. *National Professional Qualification for Headship.* It is the government's wish that eventually all applicants for their first headship would be required to have obtained the National Professional Qualification for Headship (NPQH). This is the main activity of the NCSL and has been considerably modified since its inception. In order to be accepted onto the programme, it is important that prospective applicants ensure that their present post gives them opportunities to take responsibility for a wide range of professional activities. Certainly, anyone taking up a deputy headship would be well advised to obtain the latest information from the College (the Web site address is www.ncsl.org.uk), with a view to negotiating opportunities for wide experience during the first two or three years in post. For those without this experience, it will be necessary to undertake the Access Stage; with appropriate experience, candidates can go straight to the Development Stage.

2. *Headlamp.* Newly appointed heads are given an allocation of funding, which they can spend on appropriate courses during their first two years of headship. At the time of writing there is a wide range of accredited providers (including the professional headteacher associations) with whom this money can be spent.

3. *Leadership Programme for Serving Heads.* For more experienced headteachers, there is the rather aptly named Leadership Programme for Serving Heads (LPSH). This is an intensive programme, designed to refresh existing headteachers and to update their leadership skills. Its development, planning and quality assurance is likely to remain a key part of the work of the NCSL.

The NCSL will be involved in developing programmes for school leaders, in association with a wide range of public and private providers. Its Web site (given above) will be an important source of information for school leaders.

Summary

The key elements suggested in this book so far that are necessary for personal and professional development in the teaching profession are:

- self-awareness;
- self-presentation;
- regular self-analysis of both yourself and your career;
- continuous self-education.

If these elements are well attended to, then you are likely to become – and remain – an effective educator. If you get these right, there is probably no more satisfying job.

8 *Alternative routes into teaching*

In recent years more people have been coming into teaching late, leaving early, taking career breaks and looking for post-retirement work in education. While the major part of the book – dealing with job search, application writing and interviews – is relevant to all teachers, it is worth including additional points for those who do not necessarily see teaching as a 30- to 40-year career.

Late entrants

When there is a shortage of teachers, one of the approaches often adopted by government is to try to attract people who wish to enter the profession in their 30s, 40s or 50s. Those considering such a move should be aware that HEIs (higher education institutions) have recruitment targets to meet and therefore being accepted onto a teacher training course is no guarantee of a job at the end, even if you see from the mass media that there is a severe shortage of teachers. There are certain subject areas where there is an adequate supply of teachers to meet the needs of schools. The current 'shortage' subject areas in secondary schools are mathematics, science, modern foreign languages, ICT, English, and design and technology. This situation may change. (One of the reasons for the relative difficulty of getting a secondary school post teaching history or geography is that one of the effects of the National Curriculum has been to reduce the numbers of students studying these subjects at GCSE level.)

If you are considering switching careers, the following points should help. First of all, try to spend some time in a range of types of school (primary, secondary, special), to see which environment suits you best. This is vital, as teaching a range of subjects to a class of 30 five-year-olds might be delightful to one person but may be a nightmare to those who feel more comfortable teaching a specialist subject to 14-year-olds. If you wish to teach in a secondary school – particularly an 11–16 one – you will almost certainly need a relevant qualification in a National Curriculum subject, although there is some flexibility in areas such as mathematics, science and engineering.

Once you have jumped this hurdle and still feel you would like to try teaching you need to then be sure that you actually know what teaching day in, day out – as opposed to visiting for a few days – entails. Ask teachers what they enjoy about the job and what they hate about it. In most cases the positives will outweigh the negatives, unless they are in the foolish position of battling on regardless. You need to decide if the positives would outweigh the negatives as far as you are concerned. If you are still keen, go on to the next stage!

At this point you need honest advice from those you can trust. Do you have the combination of qualities needed to teach? Recent research by PricewaterhouseCoopers shows that teachers – apart from headteachers – work comparable hours to those worked by other professionals. However, they work more intensively during term times. You need to know if this is for you or not.

There are many attributes required in good teachers. Among the most important are a genuine liking for children, a vision of what the future will be like, allied to an inner resilience to keep you going when others are losing belief. Patience and persistence are both needed in equal measure. You need to be enthusiastic, but above all you need stamina. You need to know if this is the type of person you are or not. If you do not know the answers yourself, you need to speak frankly to a close friend who does. Assuming the answer to your questions is positive, then you should approach teacher training institutions to find out the exact courses on offer.

Late entrants sometimes face problems getting a job for reasons beyond their control. Some schools have budgetary problems, which means that younger teachers are cheaper to employ for the first few years – this can make a difference of about £30,000 over seven years. However, many other schools take the view that the best person for the job is the cheapest in the long run. Those who come later into teaching have many advantages which younger applicants for posts do not. This can include experience of the wider world and/or raising children. An enthusiastic teacher of any age will have little difficulty in getting a permanent post, even in non-shortage subject areas.

Different routes into teaching

Government initiatives to encourage more graduates to consider teaching as a career have included bonuses in shortage subject areas, payment of a grant while taking a PGCE, cash to help with housing and to reward those who stay in teaching for, say, two years. The time taken to get to the threshold point on the teacher salary scale has been reduced from seven years to five, to encourage teachers to stay in teaching after their first three years.

There are also various schemes to encourage graduates to enter teaching, which are additional to the normal PGCE route. Three current schemes are detailed here. (This situation is an ever-changing one, and up-to-date information can be seen at www.canteach.gov.uk – the Web site of the Teacher Training Agency.)

Flexible postgraduate route

If you need to work while studying part-time to become a teacher, this route could provide you with what you need. It is flexible and is geared to the needs of the individual. Training is organized in modules, which start and finish at various times in the year. Evening, weekend and distance learning are all possibilities. Credit is given for such things as having trained abroad and experience in teaching in higher education and/or working in an independent school.

Employment-based routes

The Graduate and Registered Teacher Programmes (GRTP) allow people who are not yet qualified to teach and train at the same time. There are two types of programme, the Graduate Teaching Programme (GTP – about 2,000 funded places per year) and the Registered Teacher Programme (RTP – about 100 funded places per year).

The GTP involves one year of postgraduate training. It is available to those who have successfully completed at least two years of higher education and allows them to complete a degree while they train. The salary while training is currently in excess of £12,000 per year.

Fast track teaching

The Fast Track programme operates only in England. It is designed to move those with the greatest potential through teaching more quickly than usual. A bursary (currently £5,000) is available to those selected and they also qualify for double increments. Advanced Skills Teachers – who are paid more but have to undertake training in other schools for a part of the week and who are not employed for the 195 days – are eligible to go on to the Fast Track.

If you are interested in this type of programme, you are advised to get up-to-date information from www.teachernet. gov.uk/fast-trackteaching. Many of these schemes are in their infancy and may be replaced and/or added to in the light of experience.

Supply teaching

In the past, supply teaching was often undertaken by those who could not get permanent work, and by parents (usually mothers) who wished to remove themselves from the full-time arena for a period of time. The present situation is different. There are now many people, including an increasing number of younger teachers, who choose to do supply work. It is worth looking at the current benefits and drawbacks of supply teaching.

Those who choose supply teaching cite many reasons why they do so. First of all, they do not feel tied to a school or post. If they want a break, they take it. If they want to go somewhere sunny at a reasonable price (say, early December or mid-January), they can go. There is no need to give notice. They get experience in a wide variety of schools and only work in those in which they feel comfortable.

There is rarely any marking to be done, parents' evenings to attend or, even, lessons to be prepared. (Sensible supply teachers do carry a supply of pens, etc and some emergency worksheets in case the school has not organized this properly for when they arrive.) It is also possible to totally avoid OFSTED – a not unattractive proposition.

Many supply teachers will tell you that they like teaching but hate the bureaucracy and long hours spent at home working and worrying about the next week. It is also possible to combine a career in supply teaching with another pursuit, for example, writing, painting, designing Web sites, personal tutoring or even running a dry-cleaning business!

There are some drawbacks. Many supply teachers miss the continuity and sense of achievement that comes from leading a group of children on the path from ignorance to knowledge. Higher salary scales are usually not available to supply teachers, although of course the concomitant responsibility is also missing. The feeling of belonging to a team of fellow professionals, heading in the same direction towards a vision of a better future for young people, can be lacking. Career progression is also not really an option, unless supply teaching is only the preferred choice for a few years.

Secondments/interim management

While the recommendation of the James' Report a quarter of a century ago that all teachers should have regular sabbaticals has never been put into practice, there are increasingly opportunities available for secondments for teachers. Such secondments – full or part-time – may be to an LEA or a government department to help with specific projects and/or to provide advice on the implementation of a project.

There are advantages to taking a secondment, for both the teacher and his or her school. The teacher can gain experience from a wider perspective and often acquires skills (such as project or time management) that can be very useful in his or her day-to-day work. This is particularly the case for those who hold management responsibilities in schools. It can also give an individual the opportunity to have some (albeit likely to be small!) influence in the direction of education. Secondments to LEAs can also have the advantage of not requiring much, if any, additional travel.

Having a break to do something different is often the main benefit. The teacher comes back to school refreshed and rejuvenated. (This does not always apply with part-time secondments, where the secondee needs to take care not to end up even more tired than before!) The school can benefit from having a teacher with wider skills, possibly more focus, certainly more knowledge than before.

It should be noted that most secondments do not benefit the secondee financially, although the school can often benefit. The latter is particularly true if the secondee is a senior member of staff who may not need to be replaced in the short term.

Interim management is not very common in schools, although other sectors are used to the concept. Often the job – for example, being seconded into a school with particular difficulties for a set period of time – is not referred to as an interim management post, but in practice that is what if amounts to.

Those who are tempted by any form of secondment need to decide if they want to go full-time or part-time – and to be realistic about the demands of the job. They also need to do a cost-benefit analysis of the opportunity on offer. Be clear about expectations and who your line manager is. Make sure that there is a proper contract and that it makes clear what the new employer expects to pay for.

Early retirement

It has long been a tradition in some areas of employment, such as the police, for early retirement to be followed by a new career. Since the retirement age at which teachers become eligible for a full pension is 60, and the penalties for taking a pension at the age of 55 are so expensive, there are not likely to be so many teachers taking early retirement as a prelude to another career. In some ways, a three-year secondment at the age of 57 is an attractive option for some. For those who do wish to work after retiring from full-time teaching, there is a wide variety of opportunities on offer. Some are detailed here.

Supply teaching is one option that allows a gentle introduction to retirement, since many find the process of going from working flat-out in July to doing nothing after that very stressful. There are opportunities to become a part-time OFSTED inspector or a performance management consultant. Many LEAs would welcome part-time input to specific projects and/or teacher training sessions. Universities can also be useful sources of part-time work.

Writing is another source of income for many, and professional teacher organizations often welcome retired members offering their services.

If you are lucky, headhunters may approach you to take on a permanent assignment, an interim project or a series of short placements. There is nothing, of course, to stop you approaching the headhunters yourself, although you may have to pay for the privilege. Self-employment is an option, although it is important not to blow a lump sum, earned over a long career, to be gambled on an inadequately researched idea.

Whatever you want to do, there are key things to be decided. First and foremost, you need to decide why you want to continue working. For many people, retirement is something they have anticipated for a long time and they are happy to stop engaging in paid work. For others, they would like part-time paid employment. You need to be clear about what you want to do.

You need to prepare a CV. A key element will be your major achievements, particularly in the last 5–10 years of your career. You need to list your skills, particularly those that are transferable, such as project and time management.

Armed with a CV, a computer and access to the Internet, the world is your oyster. This time you have some money behind you, so you have more choice! Basically, you can do what you want to do.

Index

accreditation 98–99
Advanced Skills Teachers 5
alternative routes into teaching 109–16
application, making an 21, 22, 24, 25, 27
application forms 49–50
appointment to a post 93
assessment centres 87
assistant heads 17, 102–03

career appraisal 9
career objectives 1, 2, 4
challenge 4
choosing the right school 5, 81–82
closing dates 24
courses 97–98
curriculum vitae (CV) 11, 13, 22, 25, 27–47, 50, 69, 116

deadlines 11
debriefing 94
deputy headships 18–19, 52, 54, 63, 84–85
   as a step to headships 17
   primary schools 36–38, 63, 65–66
   responsibilities of 102–03
   secondary schools 38–41, 65–66
dress code for interviews 76–77

employment offer 16
ethos of a school 8, 81–82
expenses, interview 81–82
experience 9, 41
experienced teachers, career objectives of 4

fast-track teaching 112
filling vacancies 24

good teachers, attributes of 110–11

handwritten letters 55
Headlamp 106
headship 20, 42–47, 84
   applications for 54, 56, 69–74
   key relationships 105
   leadership, development of 105–07
   prior experience of appointees 17
   qualifications for headteachers 106

headship *continued*
  qualities needed   66–67,
    103–04
  recruitment   68, 85–87
  updating   105
hours of work   110

independent schools   8
interim management   114–15
interviews   75–94
  formal   89–90
  getting   49–74
  informal   89
  types of questions   91–92
interview tips   90
in-tray exercises   88

job details   21
job search   11–20

late entrants to teaching
    109–11
Leadership Programme for
    Serving Heads (LPSH)
    106
leadership teams   101–02
letters of application   13, 21,
    22, 23, 53–73

management   4, 14, 19,
    82–84, 100–01
money   5
motivation   3

National College for School
    Leadership (NCSL)
    105–07

National Professional
    Qualification for
    Headship (NPQH)   106
new teachers   1, 12, 30–33, 82
notice   11

performance management
    9, 53, 99
personal development   35,
    95–107
personal strengths   2
planning   1, 9, 12, 16
postgraduate teacher training
    111–12
primary schools   14, 15, 20
  deputy headship   17, 18,
    36–38, 63–65, 74
  headship   17, 18, 42–44
  posts in   15
private life   3, 4
professional development
    96–97, 105
promotion   5, 8, 14, 15, 17, 41
  experienced teachers   4
  first steps to   32–36
  new teachers   2
  opportunities, affected by
    school   7
  those not wanting, career
    development for   95
  what does it entail?   99
psychometric tests   100

referees   32, 35, 40, 51–53
resignation dates   13, 75
retirement   115–16
routes into teaching   111–14

sabbaticals 96
secondary schools 14, 15, 19, 20, 58–63
  deputy headship 17, 18, 38–41
  headship 17, 18, 20, 44–46, 70–75
  posts in 15
secondments 17, 114–15
selection criteria 51
self-awareness 3
self-fulfilment 5
senior management teams 101–02
shortage subjects 13, 109
status 5

strengths 2, 3, 4
succession management 87
supply teaching 113–14

testimonials 53
Times Educational Supplement 11, 96

upper pay spine 5, 99

vacancies 11

weaknesses, analysing one's 2, 3, 4
word-processing an application letter 55